A
Time
Well Spent

A
Time
Well Spent

A *Biography of Jerome Brody*

Lawrence S. Freundlich

Welcome Rain Publishers

Library of Congress Cataloging-in-Publication data
available from the Publisher.

Direct any inquiries to
Welcome Rain Publishers LLC,
225 West 35th Street, Suite 100
New York, NY 10001

ISBN 1-56649-173-8

Designed by Tony Meisel
Manufactured in the United States
of America by BLAZE I.P.I.

First Edition: September 2000
1 3 5 7 9 10 8 6 4 2

Contents

Foreword

In 1963, when Jerome Brody was forced out of Restaurant Associates, the company was poised for its greatest financial success ever. For sixteen years, Brody, along with his handpicked associates, had run his in-law's restaurant company with close to no input.

In his first year at Dartmouth, Brody had married school friend Grace, the daughter of Abraham F. Wechsler, himself the son of Philip Wechsler, who was the founder of The Wechsler Coffee Company, a leading coffee importer, and who was the unhappy owner of Rikers Cafeterias. The cafeteria chain, which his in-laws insisted Brody manage when he returned as a 24-year-old B-24 bomber pilot from a four-year stint in the Army Air Corps, consisted of twenty Rikers coffee shops in New York, which in 1942 were merged with five Silver's cafeterias and a few Topps restaurants, which Wechsler had acquired earlier.

This was the melancholy hodgepodge that originally bore the Restaurant Associates (RA) name. The entire operation was on the verge of failure—its management neither capable nor willing to provide the capital and managerial commitment necessary to turn the operation into a success.

Brody did rejuvenate some of the shops, but many others were hopelessly outdated, unable to compete with such highly organized and well-financed systems as those created by Horn & Hardart. With the Wechsler purse strings drawn tight, Brody needed to look beyond Rikers to find landlords who would bear the initial start up costs of new and different kinds of food ventures.

The Port of New York Authority became one such partner, and the result was food concessions at Newark Airport, which among other profit centers resulted in the Newarker restaurant, which was Restaurant Associates' first venture into full-service, table-cloth dining. Coinciding with the Newark Airport ventures, and, again, with his eye on keeping the initial need for capital to a minimum, Brody directed RA into the food-service management business, which yielded immediate cash-flow credibility. Brody bid on the section of Thruway between Syracuse and Buffalo, and the New York State Thruway Authority granted Brody the concession, preferring his plan to those personally proposed by Howard Johnson and Bill Marriott. Brody's reputation as a creative and practical financial strategist grew.

Brody's key financial insight into growing and evolving RA was a strategy by which landlords in need of aggressive restaurant clients with sound management plans contributed the retail space and the capital for opening construction and equipment in return for percentages of the gross and the prestige and traffic the restaurants would give to the buildings which housed them. Thus, with little working capital, Brody was eventually able to place Restaurant Associates in first-rate locations, create a presence in the restaurant world out of proportion to the company's wealth, and give it a clout, which considering its humble origins was all the more remarkable.

By1955, under Brody's tightly managed and imaginative

guidance, RA operated more than sixty restaurants serving 16,000,000 meals yearly. Aspiring upwards from the basic end of the restaurant business, Brody created a group of world-renowned restaurants. Noted as much for their opulent beauty as for their cuisine, these restaurants probably did more to raise the standards of American fine dining than any other single factor in the post-War era and made New York City, for the first time in its history, an international food capital.

Not only did the Forum of the Twelve Caesars, La Fonda del Sol, and the Four Seasons put American restaurant dining on a par with the best of Europe, they became meeting places for celebrities, celebrity seekers, politicians, expense account kings of the communications world, visiting royalty, socialites, stars of Broadway and Hollywood, and society and gossip columnists who stalked them. Brody's grand visions, coupled with his meticulous attention to detail, allowed his design collaborators to create the model for a revolution in dining aesthetics and inalterably raised the expectations under which knowledgeable Americans expected to dine.

By 1961, Brody had already carved out his niche in restaurant history as the man who combined the economy of chain operations with the connoisseur's insistence upon sparing no expense to produce the perfect meal in the perfect setting. His staffs of corporate and restaurant executives were the best in the business. The gross sales for Brody restaurants in 1961 was $25 million. When he took over the restaurant division from the Wechslers, it was $5 million and showing net losses.

Restaurant Associates had become the pre-eminent name in the restaurant industry. And, the Four Seasons, leased and financed by Seagram, with the personal backing of Sam and Edgar Bronfman, designed by Philip Johnson, and widely thought of as the number one dining address in America, had become the crown jewel in an empire which the food world thought of as Brody's own.

That the Wechslers (including his wife's 40%) owned Brody's empire was hardly known at all. Even when the Wechslers declined to invest in ventures Brody deemed necessary, he arranged the financing himself, often despite the Wechslers' masochistic obstructionism, but always to the benefit of RA. And for as long as Brody ran the business and was married to a Wechsler that was fine with them—or at least tolerable.

In 1963, Brody became the first foreigner ever to be granted equity in a French gambling company. It was the most important deal Brody had pulled off to date. The acquisition, a stake in the French hotel and casino at Divonne-les-Bains, would have dramatically increased RA's wealth and cash flow, opening the doors to major bank financing and European expansion. The Wechslers had refused to put up money for the venture. Shortly after Brody himself had arranged the financing for the purchase, Abe Wechsler asked for Brody's resignation, refusing his offer to buy Wechsler's controlling share in RA.

The rupture coincided with the acrimonious end of his troubled 22-year marriage to Grace Wechsler; Wechsler blood was speaking louder than money. Without control, Brody would have been facing hostile partners, and, for the first time ever, an active Board whose judgment Brody did not trust or respect. There was nothing for Brody to do other than acquiesce in his forced resignation, leaving behind him, at the moment of its full flowering, the most important fine dining assemblage in America.

This book has two main divisions. The first concerns Brody's shaping of Restaurant Associates until the time of his resignation. The second tells the story of his career after his marriage to Sumatra-born and Ceylon-educated Marlene Gray, who brought into his life a love, which by his own reckoning, was more important than anything he had achieved in business.

Brody and Gray's life together has a dream quality to it. They turned a small upstate New York farm into Gallagher's Stud, where, as neophyte Angus breeders, they almost instantly produced world champions. With that venture behind them and with little to no experience, they next immersed themselves in the glamorous and high-risk world of thoroughbred racing and commercial breeding. The results of these adventures produced Grade 1 champions on the track and a broodmare program among the best in the country, one that earned Brody the New York Thoroughbred Breeders Breeder of the Year Award.

Brody's restaurant life did not end with his leaving RA. In fact, in his late seventies, Brody is in the midst of a restaurant franchising operation that promises to become his most lucrative restaurant enterprise. And although his unceremonious ouster from Restaurant Associates in the early '60s when the empire he had created was at its most glittering was a bitter pill, Brody's new life as an animal breeder and restaurateur has been the best revenge.

After the RA split, Brody managed the Rainbow Room for eleven years, bringing to one of the world's most beautiful restaurant locations the shine and glamour it had gradually been losing. His subsequent re-entry into the restaurant business acquainted Brody with hard times. Investments in the trendy Raffles Club in the Sherry Netherland, and in L'Étoile, where, in his own words, "We lost our shirts," left him bruised, but not defeated. Brody rebounded spectacularly with the revitalization of two landmark restaurants, one in serious decline, Gallagher's, and one bankrupt, in disrepair, and chained shut, the Grand Central Oyster Bar. He turned them into culinary and financial successes. They flourish today as they never have before, having become the flagships of a growing franchising empire.

In the glory days of the Four Seasons, La Fonda del Sol, the Forum of the Twelve Caesars, and Divonne, when Brody's establishments were the touchstones of taste and glamour, Brody was well-served by a tremendously intelligent, imaginative and dedicated management team. But after his departure from RA, history has sometimes credited Brody's own achievements to some of his former lieutenants, often at their own instigation. But Brody's own unique entrepreneurial courage and know-how, his ability to pick the right managers, his hands-on attention to details both minute and grand, coupled with his master builder's sense of restaurant design were at the center of RA's success. Without him, there would not be a Restaurant Associates story worth telling.

Introduction

Water, water, every where
Nor any drop to drink

In the years after the war, New York cuisine was no better than the rest of the country's. For the most part, what it had in ethnic variety was obviated by how naively or uncaringly it was prepared. London, at least, could blame its blasphemous food on the War; New York could not. What's more, few people seemed to care. The *New York Times* did not even review restaurants until 1964.

Ask for restaurant memories from cosmopolitan New Yorkers of a certain age and they remember how boring and undistinguished the food was, but they usually have a demurrer. It goes something like this: "Of course, the food in general was awful. New Yorkers didn't know about French cuisine and/or fresh produce. They didn't yet care. But, of course there was "Chambord." Amid the culinary desert, there was Chambord, NewYork's homage to Parisian *cordon bleu* perfection, serving to a clientele of New York's 400 classically prepared *haute cuisine*, as much a delight to the eye as to the palate.

There were other good restaurants in the City, but they were few and they were not cosmopolitan. Gage and Tollner's on Fulton Street in Brooklyn masterfully served the specialties of the

Chesapeake. Peter Luger's Steak House, also in Brooklyn, served, then as now, as good a steak as the planet provides, but on a menu almost entirely dedicated to steak. Luchow's on 14th Street served mounds of rollicking German sausages and game in an atmosphere as subtle as October Fest in Bavaria.

Italian restaurants pretty much meant Sicilian restaurants. The flavor was garlic; the bread was anonymous, as was the cheese. The red wine was blue-collar Chianti, the white, Sicilian all-purpose *pinot grigio*. The veal and chicken, delivered by generic coops who bought their produce from farms raising the animals on God knows what chemicals, and the fish, whether fresh from Sheepshead Bay or the Fulton Market, was more often than not overcooked into vapidity, as was the custom of the day. To order *al dente* pasta marked you as an exotic. Green salads seemed familiar, because you could have ordered similar ones at any cafeteria. The decor was often a cousin's primitive mural of Napoli and red-and-white checkered tableclothes. And yet people flocked to Patsy's and to the Grotto Azzuro and loved them. Lidia Bastianich's Felidia and Tony May's San Domenico were many years in the future. America's taste buds were primitive.

Ruby Foo's was the Chinese hot spot. But the repertoire was strictly Cantonese, and most of the customers had no suspicion that there was anything else Chinese worth eating. Yes, there was a time when people ordered egg roll, egg drop soup, chow mein, egg foo young, lobster Cantonese, and brown rice with overcooked pork and overcooked vegetables. Dessert was a Libby's ring of pineapple and a fortune cookie. The adventurous could go to Chinatown, and if they survived the crowds and the language barrier, find themselves choosing among dozens of "authentic" Chinese restaurants, all serving the same food as their neighbor, raising the suspicion that they all shared the same sauce pot. The day of the Mandarin Palace, Szechwan Balcony, and

Golden Unicorn was decades in the future.

How the food world has changed. By 2000 New York City had become one of the great restaurant capitals of the world. Zagat's Restaurant Survey reviews one thousand eight-hundred-and-eight restaurants . Specialty food shops are everywhere, serving up all of the world's delicacies—smoked meats and fishes, exotic sauces, rare mushrooms and princely *hors d'oeuvres*. Fresh farm produce including raddichio and leeks, fiddlehead ferns, *haricot verts*, bok choy, tangelos, pomegranates, and mangoes, are widely available in and out of season. Dozens of specialty bakeries and confectioners are ready from early morning to late evening with their fresh baguettes, raisin scones, Linzer tortes and Napoleons, raspberry, prune, and apricot rugalach, oatmeal chocolate chip cookies and truffles coated in white chocolate.

At the best fish restaurants, Dover sole is served fresh daily, having been caught that day in the English Channel and packed in ice in time to make the morning Concorde to JFK. Salmon from Norway and from Washington State, crab from the Chesapeake, stripers from Montauk, catfish from Mississippi, abalone from California, oysters from Chile, roughy from Australia, trout from the Rockies and whitefish from the Great Lakes appear regularly on dozens of restaurant menus.

New York is an international gourmet capital now. Apart from the food itself, restaurant design, interior decor, and great expense involve a cadre of superb architects, designers and financiers in such eye-catchers as "21," the food halls of Dean & DeLuca, Buzz O'Keefe's Water Club, Le Cirque 2000 in Villard House, Windows on the World, the Ocean Club, and the Gramercy Tavern off Park Avenue South. In New York, the world is your oyster or your dim sum or your sauerbraten. Distinguished New York restaurants serve Chinese, Vietnamese, Tibetan, and Indian specialties. It is possible to argue that one can eat French food as well in New York as in Paris, perhaps with the exception of Paris's 4-star elite. New York's Italian restaurants while paying homage to Sicily, Bologna and Venezia, enter into equal battle with them, not in small part because the quality of meat and produce available to New York restaurateurs. And the pasta, be it either made fresh daily on premises or bought from Chinese bakers who have made it hours before is only a small step below the standards of Bologna. Latin American food abounds, as does the food of Indian, Eastern European, and all the countries of Indo-China.

By 2000 New York seems a little food mad. Elite private caterers, world-class produce vendors, gourmet specialty shops, boutique fish mongers, and prime butchers and game purveyors, churn out 100's of millions of dollars of business in a market that gets bigger every year. High-end restaurant entrepreneurs such as Alan Stillman (the Manhattan Ocean Club), Drew Nieporent (TriBeCa Grill), Danny Meyer (Gramercy Tavern), Michael Whitman (Windows on the World) finance and manage multiple restaurant groups, all competing at the highest level of decor, expense, and culinary excellence. And the trend is bullish.

Reviews appear in the *New York Times*, *The Post*, *The Daily News* and *Newsday*. Cable features the 24-hour Food Channel. The Manhattan Chapter of the American Institute of Wine and Food holds twenty-five gourmet events each year for its 850-members, who are invited to a significant hostelry or hotel to dine and sample one special aspect of the world of cuisine, ranging from rice to game, from the cheeses of the world to truffles, from champagne to microbeers, from peppers to *pate*. On clement weekends, lines stretch down the block in front of bruncheon restaurants featuring croissants, and eggs benedict, andouille sausages, baguettes of melted mozzarella, sun-dried tomatoes and balsamic vinegar, mango, banana, strawberry, orange slices, and blueberry fruit salads, washed down with a mind-boggling choice of specialty coffee blends, and sweetened with unbleached sugar-in-the-raw.

The newsstand on the north balcony of Grand Central Station offers *Food Arts, Gourmet, Saveur, Food and Wine,* and *Nation's Restaurant News*. Celebrated chefs earn $300,000 per year. A year's tuition at the Culinary Institute of America is $20,000 plus. Food catalogue sales are soaring.

And if you choose not to eat out, you can order in. The motto of Angelo Vivolo's Cucina Vivolo, the take-out adjunct to the regular restaurant is "Take the Best of Vivolo's Home with You." New Yorkers are so attuned to good food that many New York's fine restaurants deliver food to the homes of the exhausted refugees of Wall Street. We are not talking about pizza, quick Chinese, and deli, but a porterhouse from Smith & Wolensky, a veal picatta from Vivolo's, a red snapper amandine from the Gramercy Tavern, oyster stew from the Grand Central Oyster Bar,and this accompanied by a full array of appetizers, vegetables, soups, and dessert. Were you to chose more ordinary fare, you could take out the world's best sandwiches from Todaro's, the most luxurious salads from Zabar's, and the pick of the world's best cheeses and breads from Dean & DeLuca. New York is now a gourmet delight, a flowering garden of the world's comestibles.

How did we go from food desert to gourmet cornucopia? What instigated the change? The answer can in large part, be found by examining the development of Jerry Brody's high-end restaurants.

College
Marriage
War

"I'd like to be a millionaire." Jerome Brody
Senior Year, Ethical Culture School

Perhaps Jerry Brody's taste for business can be traced back to the considerable wealth and success his father Jacob (known as "Jac") enjoyed in the retail men's hat business. In the 1920s, Jac Brody had made a fortune and, in 1928 had sold his company to the Hat Corporation of America. Life at home for the Brodys was free and easy. But 1929 came along and, like most everyone else, Jac was hard hit, especially since much of his money was invested in real estate.

Jac re-entered the retail men's hat business by buying control of a successful retail men's hat chain, Young's, which he ran with great success during and after World War II, turning it into a 50-store chain and becoming an acknowledged big shot in the thriving men's hat business.

Jac devoted his life to running his business, and provided Jerome with a model of total dedication to the operations of his stores and to the well-being of his key employees and associates. In the 1950's, when Jac divested himself of Young's, he sold the stores to his managers, and continued to visit each of them, unwilling to cut the connection which had given central meaning to his life.

Jerome Brody was born in New York City, in 1922, a child of the Depression. His older sister Ellie developed serious mastoid problems in infancy. Her mother and father feared for her life, and, in fact, the doctor consoled her parents by assuring them that although they would lose Ellie, they were young and would have other children. But the Brodys were not about to abandon Ellie to her disease. They spent their life savings on surgery and aftercare, and were deeply humiliated having to move in with Mrs. Brody's parents, when they were unable to afford rent.

For the next three years, Ellie was often in agony. She was an ordeal to her parents. All the love which Ellie's distress made so trying to give to her, was given Jerry on his birth. Ellie, now in her early eighties, speculates that her brother's lifelong self-assurance and sense of empowerment can be traced back to those early years.

Because Jac's fortunes eventually soared, the children were brought up in a privileged milieu, but their parents, who never forgot their days of poverty, made the children aware of economic contrasts. In the 1930's, Brody could sympathize with the Depression's criticisms of the capitalist system, which was in shambles.

When Brody returned from World War II, he witnessed the painful failure of his father's hat business. In one of those epochal changes of fashion, men, who had been wearing hats for decades, suddenly stopped wearing them at all. All the hat companies failed. By the time Brody was ready to start his own business career, he had seen the failure of economic systems and financial strongholds; the hard realism it instilled in him characterized his way of evaluating and running businesses ever after.

During the Depression, young Jerry attended the highly idealistic Ethical Culture School, as did Ellie, filled then as now with the scions of New York's well-to-do and cultured families.

Jac Brody was a strong believer in education. In fact, years later, when Ellie married Eddie Roberts, Jac insisted that Eddie attend Harvard Business School and paid for his education. That example of paternal generosity rubbed off on Brody, when it came time for his grandchildren to be educated.

Just before matriculation, the Head Master of the school, The Reverend Algernon Black, whose presence was so magisterial that his own son, David, admits to having confused him with God, asked the graduating seniors about their ambitions. Voiced among the expected aspirations—lawyer, doctor, social worker, scientist, investment banker—was Jerry's honest, if startling, "I'd like to be a millionaire"—during the Depression, an answer as unfashionable as it was unlikely. Childhood and adolescent clues that Jerry's path to those improbable millions would be through the restaurant business are few.

At Ethical Culture, Jerry had reasonable social prominence and he was a better than average student. He played on the varsity soccer and baseball teams, and, at a long-limbed and muscular 6' 1", was captain of the basketball team. He had a special girlfriend, who also attended Ethical Culture, Grace Wechsler, and when Jerry was accepted at Dartmouth, his memories of her followed him.

Grace Wechsler, like her future husband, came from a wealthy Jewish background. Her father Abe had always been somewhat overshadowed by his father Philip, who had gained the family's acceptance in the upper levels of the Jewish community. Along with his partner, Nat Schulman, Philip had turned investments in the real estate business into a finance company, which owned such celebrated Central Park West residential landmarks as the Beresford and the San Remo. Problems arose when Philip tried to integrate his son Abe into the real estate operation and discovered that Nat Schulman found it difficult to get along with

Abe. Philip and Nat eventually dissolved the partnership.

During the Depression, however, the Abe Wechsler family had done well, especially in comparison with some of their once wealthy friends, who had suffered badly. During these hard times, Abe Wechsler was able and willing to lend a helping hand, and he had genuine reason to feel his importance in their lives. However, when the War was finally over, these old friends recovered remarkably quickly, not only re-establishing their fortunes, but in the boom economy of the 50s, becoming tycoons, leaving Abe Wechsler in their dust. This did not sit well with Abe, and this undertone of envy influenced Grace to care over much about moving in the right circles. For Jerry Brody, consumed as he would become by his business life, Grace's social anxieties were foreign, and her country club, suburban life-style alien to his interests and temperament

Pearl Harbor got in the way of Jerry Brody's sophomore year at college, but the coming of war was not his only extracurricular distraction. During his sophomore year at Dartmouth, Brody did two things a lot of young collegians were doing: he signed up in the Army Air Force and he got married. As impulsive as such a move might at first seem, in those days, Brody recalls "The movies were filled with stories of people who went off to war and got killed, so they got married first."

World War II was the last war Americans were to be united in their righteous determination to defeat evil. Brody remembers how admired he felt in his shiny dress uniform, wearing the wings of which he was so proud, when, on his last leave before being shipped to advanced training, he and Grace attended the gala Broadway premier of the play, "Winged Victory." Walking among that stylish, patriotic crowd, with his new wife on his arm and an heroic mission before him, all was great expectations.

Brody's first year at Dartmouth had been academically

satisfactory. However, his work at the college newspaper, "The Dartmouth," commanded a full commitment of his time and talents. For Brody it was a great experience, and, by his sophomore year, he became business manager of the newspaper. Although "The Dartmouth" was a college newspaper, it was the only daily in town, and its features and the local Associated Press stories were read avidly by town and gown alike.

The war had caused the academic program to accelerate, and until the boys were called up, they were driven hard. Due to academics, Brody was rewarded a semester at Dartmouth's prestigious Tuck School of Business Administration, but while there, he still had to keep the newspaper functioning. The Tuck School gave him experience in practical business techniques that helped him through the newspaper's financial crisis.

Because of enlistment, there were far fewer of Brody's newspaper colleagues to keep the paper functioning. Some of the old policies had to be redirected if the paper was to remain solvent. It had been common practice for the local merchants to purchase advertising space not for cash but for due bills or trade credits. But now that had become impossible, and so Brody went to visit the key merchants in Hanover personally and asked them to support the war properly by paying cash for their ads, which they did. That a sophomore inexperienced in the world of business had the composure and self-confidence to make such a move successfully is an augury of Brody's later straightforward boldness in problem-solving.

Brody was able to finish the semester at Tuck, but in February of 1943, he started Air Force pilot training, which began in cold and nasty Atlantic City, which had been converted into a basic training center for the Army. He stayed there for two months.

By that time all the services had more men than they could

train and had to devise ways to keep its soldiers involved. The Air Force had a program called "college training," where selected groups were sent off to various colleges for what was supposed to be two months. Brody's group of New England Ivy Leaguers, including the captain of the Harvard basketball team, was gratuitously sent to Birmingham Southern College. But, when Brody got there, he scored high on his advanced placement examination, and, therefore, left after a month.

Next he was shipped to a classification center in Nashville, Tennessee, and in the six weeks he was there, he was selected for pilot training, and then sent off again to a shrunken imitation of West Point, at Maxwell Field, Montgomery, Alabama. By that time it was summer. Here the trainees were put through arduous physical tests, including long cross-country runs, and emotional hazing. Drills were done at attention, but so was eating. If you survived, you were introduced to ground school, which took two months.

Brody thrived. He went next to primary flight school in Clarksdale, Mississippi, where, finally, he and his group began to fly. The first crisis for the neophyte flyers was intentionally arranged. All the flyers were required to fly solo within their ten hours of flying time. To Brody, it sounded like the height of achievement, when, during his eighth hour, his instructor said, "You take it up," and got out of the plane.

Brody taxied out the plane and began to sing at the top of his lungs. He even managed to take off, fly around, and land. From that time on, his flying time was almost all solo; he even learned aerial acrobatics. It had been only two months, but he and his class had passed through a key phase; the men who did not solo "washed out," and were sent to navigation and bombardier school.Brody and the others became aviation cadets. Each was required to have two years of college, but during World War II, the level of volunteerism was so high, that even if the Air Force had demanded college graduates, the ranks of aviator candidates would have been full.

Then came two months in Greenville, Mississippi at basic flying school, and here the candidates were given the experience of bigger airplanes. Brody's most memorable test came during his "instrument check" rides, where, with an instructor monitoring performance, the cadet flew the plane under a hood which covered the cockpit and prevented the student from seeing out. Only the instruments were visible, as the instructor made staccato demands to the pilot to make certain kinds of turns, to climb at a certain rate, and to descend. Brody knew that his instrument check pilot was the famous musician, Larry Clinton, but it did not take Clinton's fame in the musical world to make the experience unforgettable.

At this point, the officers divided the men into fighter pilots and bomber pilots, based mostly on their physical dimensions. Brody went into the bomber group and proceeded to an advanced, twin-engine training base at Georgefield, Illinois, where upon completion, he was able, finally, to wear the Air Force wings.

As Grace followed Jerry from base to base, life on the move for a woman concerned that her young husband would soon see combat, was a strain. But, even without the spectre of combat looming, there was reason for wives to worry about death or injury. Those early Air Force Training camps were plagued with fatal accidents. The Brodys, who would spend time on numerous airbases, were never on one where there was not at least one fatal accident a month and usually more.

The marriage was already troubled. Grace complained that their physical relationship was not exciting enough. The complaint was allowed to linger in the half-darkness. The matter of sexual incompatibility continued in secret throughout most of their marriage, until, after many years, they would seek satisfaction outside it.

Brody's first assignment as a bomber pilot was at bombardier school in Albuquerque, New Mexico. Brody flew student bombardiers and their instructors, in a small Cessna bomber trainer, in daylight and at night, over ranges that had been established in the desert to test their ability to annihilate targeted shacks.

It was in Albuquerque that Grace gave birth to their first daughter, Ricki. From that time forward the relationship between Grace and Jerry centered on the new baby. While Brody had the intense involvement and the camaraderie of his fellow flyers, Grace's life as a young, city woman used to the better things of life was, perforce, conventional, lonely, and, probably not much more than bearable. Ricki became her best companion.

Brody was next sent to B-24 pilot school at Smyrna, Tennessee. As had become the routine, this training session was to last two months, but during the end of the session there, the European war ended. The amount of disorganization escalated as all the pilots hurried to get in the minimum of four hours a month flight time required to get the "flight tag," which would earn them a 50% bonus. There were even more accidents than usual. But with an end to the war in sight, there was a widespread feeling that they were doing nothing useful.

After a month in Smyrna, Brody was assigned to gunnery school in Harlingen, Texas, about 20 miles north of Brownsville. Brody had already logged more than 500 hours of flying time. Here in a program called B-29 Airplane Commander, Brody would fly B-24s, which had been converted to carry remote-controlled B-29 gunnery equipment. They were the first bombers to have pressurized cabins.

On a typical mission the student gunners, two gunnery instructors, a newly commissioned co-pilot, and the airplane commander would fly out over the Gulf and rendezvous with a P-51 "enemy" from a satellite base. The skin of the target adversary was electrified to register electronically hits from the frangible bullets of the bomber's guns. It was rather like a modern Top Gun computer game, with the high score getting the win. Often, when Brody's bomber was on its way to such an encounter, the self-important commander would lose interest in the proceedings and turn the radio on to a commercial station for his listening pleasure. On one of those mornings, there was a discussion about some crazy kind of bomb that had just been dropped on the Japanese. The commander of the bomber was Brody. The city was Hiroshima.

Brody had gained favor with the brass, in part because of his cavalier spirit, but mostly because he was a skilled and fearless pilot. Returning from one of his P-51 electronic Top Gun missions, the rain was pouring down onto the landing strip. Brody expected the tower to order him to circle around for a while until conditions improved. But this time the tower remained silent. Being young and macho, Brody came in for a landing on a runway that was covered with about 3/4" of water. The landing was perfect, and word went out from the flight run that Brody was a hot shot. Further increasing his standing within the cadre were his good relations with the base commander, who requested that Brody fly him to various cities in the area when the commander's duties were required. The commander suggested that Brody stay in the Air Force, and he promised to help further his career. Brody listened, but a career in the Air Force was not whar he had in mind.

The commander put Brody in charge of consolidating under one roof a processing center to coordinate all the orders the men needed to clear from the time they arrived at the base until the time that they left. Brody had under his command the sergeants from all those departments, from medical to personnel. Brody organized his assignment so successfully that when the bomb finally dropped on Japan, his group was cleared for return home. Speaking to his sergeant in personnel, Brody requested that his discharge papers be moved from underneath the pile to the top. Were it not for a hurricane, Brody would have been out within the month.

It was one of those fierce hurricanes, which plague the Brownsville area. Brody and a co-pilot were given the assignment to move the aircraft out of danger. His co-pilot was fresh from combat duty; he liked to wear his decorations on his flight gear. It was just a one-day assignment to fly aircraft out of danger, wait out the storm in Oklahoma City and come back.

The three men, the pilot, flight engineer, and co-pilot, started down the runway. The instrumentation in the plane was as primitive as the airport itself; there was no assistance for instrument landing. The ceiling was down to about 500 feet as they started down the runway. The air speed indicator rose to 100 and stopped. It would move no higher. Since the B-24 takes off at 130 miles an hour, Brody poked his co-pilot in the shoulder and laughingly said something like, "Ha, ha, look at that." The combat veteran turned slightly gray. But Brody, who had more than 300 hours in B-24s, was familiar enough with the plane to know that it would take off when it reached the right speed, and besides, there was nothing he could do about it.

Once aloft, Brody called back to the tower to say that given the state of their air speed indicator, he was not going to Oklahoma City. Given the primitive state of the plane's instrumentation, Brody needed the air speed indicator to tell him whether the plane was climbing or descending: down, the plane picked up speed; up, the plane slowed. He would have to depend on visual advice from the tower and his own eyes.

Brody made a pattern around the field, and he broke out to land. At about 500 feet, he saw that he was missing the runway, so he brought the plane back up into the clouds and made another pass, hoping to give himself plenty of distance to correct. He was now faced with landing an airplane that stalled out at speeds below 125 miles an hour. The malfunctioning air speed indicator no longer went that high. But Brody brought the plane down with no problem. By that time his combat hardened co-pilot had changed from gray to white. It was the only problem Brody ever had with his aircraft. Many of his colleagues had not been so lucky and were dead.

At last, Brody went to Fort Dix, New Jersey to be honorably discharged. The commander of his Harlingen base was shocked that Brody was getting out so fast.

Now Brody thought of the various choices that awaited him. He could return to Dartmouth on the GI Bill, he could join his father in the hat business or he could pursue a profession. Those were the questions facing the Brodys when they returned to New York City—all those questions plus where to find a place to live in a city where, in the hyper-glut of returning veterans, it was next to impossible to find one.

Rikers Cafeterias

Brody went to work for his father at the hat company, while the young couple, unable to find an apartment, lived with Grace's father, Abe.

It was a hard time. As much as he loved his father, it was clear to both of them that the hat business was dead. Even the Adams Hat Company ("I go for a man who wears an Adams hat") was in collapse. It was logical for Brody to find a profession, and his decision to attend Columbia Law School, although he was uncomfortable with the idea of becoming a schoolboy again, was at first applauded by both his father and Abe Wechsler.

The night before Brody's enrollment, his father-in-law withdrew his support. He was frantic: "You can't go to law school, you *have to* come down and join me in my coffee business." Brody did what Abe demanded.

The coffee company was run separately from the restaurant division, and it was Philip, not his son Abe, who had interest in the restaurants. Abe was not about to step in and take matters into his own hands.

The reason for Wechsler's frenzy was that, within 2 years, fatal heart attacks had felled three presidents in a row of Rikers

Cafeterias. Wechsler was left holding a $200,000 overdraft at the bank and with no one to keep the stores from closing permanently. At least the young, fit Brody seemed unlikely to die on him.

Before moving to the Rikers end of the business, Brody worked for the parent Wechsler Coffee Company, and very early on became involved in a scenario which would reveal the fracture in loyalties which alienated Brody and Abe Wechsler.

Brody knew that the Rain or Shine Box Lunch Company of Newark, New Jersey, which sold fast food lunches and coffee to workers at factory sites, could become a major customer for Wechsler coffee. Brody called the company and arranged to meet with the owner of Rain or Shine (whose name was coincidentally also Brody) and his son Martin. Rain and Shine, did in fact become an important customer of Wechsler.

Later on, when Brody had moved on to become RA's prominent restaurateur, charge of the Rain or Shine was given to Jimmy Slater, who had married Grace Brody's sister, Elaine. A strong bond grew up between Jimmy Slater and Martin Brody (no relation to Jerome) of Rain or Shine, and in 1961, Slater and Martin Brody did a successful IPO to create a company, which financed vending machine companies. It was that company which financed the merger of Waldorf Systems and Restaurant Associates of which Martin Brody became chairman. In contemplating the $35 million investment in Waldorf, Jerry Brody's advice and consent would not be sought and was a herald of his coming dismissal.

In the short time Jerry Brody worked for the coffee company, he had become uncomfortable with some of Wechsler's business tactics. One of them was Wechsler's practice of lending money to restaurants, which resulted in getting Wechsler coffee into those restaurants. Some of those loans were made to very shaky enterprises. When they failed, it was not unusual for Wechsler to acquire these companies in bankruptcy proceedings with money provided by the Wechsler Coffee Company. Such tactics were not illegal; however, in Brody's eyes, they were unethical. One of the distinctions between banking and loan sharking is that bankers consider failed loans failures of their own judgment in assessing the credit worthiness of the borrower, not opportunities to benefit from the failure.

Brody's discomfort was such that he felt like parting ways with his father-in-law. It is a sad irony that if Brody had followed his instincts, his painful marriage to Grace would have ended sooner. Concomitantly, the long simmering differences between Brody and Abe Wechsler, culminating sixteen years later in Brody's ouster from Restaurant Associates, would not have been granted long life. But then again, neither would Brody as son-in-law have created the most admired restaurant company in America.

Wechsler did not know how or choose to learn how to run the restaurant business. His dire view of the restaurant business had been permanently shaped by his having watched several of the restaurants to whom he sold coffee during the Depression go bankrupt. The only reason the family owned them was to satisfy their debts. So, in 1947, twenty-five-year-old Jerome volunteered himself for work in an industry for which his father-in-law had no respect. As previously noted, Wechsler's last three restaurant presidents had died of heart attacks: Isadore Silver, in 1946, Sam Scheinberg, and Abe's brother, Eddie, in the subsequent months. If for no other reason than his vitality, Abe made Brody president of the restaurant division.

Finally the young Brodys were able to rent a gracious flat in the magnificent Beresford Apartments, an old Central Park West holding of Philip Wechsler's former real estate company. Grace gave birth to the Brodys second daughter Kathy. While the Brodys were at the Beresford, and Brody was running the Restaurant Company, Philip Wechsler died.

In anticipation of his own death, and in order to save estate taxes, Philip had turned 52% of the stock in the Wechsler Coffee Company over to his son Abe and to Abe's brothers and sisters. However, in deed and appearance, Philip behaved as if he still ran the show.

Although the young Brody found it awkward to plead his own case in front of his father-in-law, Brody asked for participation in the stock redistribution, which he based on the 52% Abe had received from Philip. Brody wanted 52% of the stock in the separate restaurant company, "Restaurant Associates."

Wechsler was not unsympathetic, but following the example of his father's tactic of skipping generations for tax reasons, gave 42% of the RA stock to Grace and the children and 10% to Brody. The other 48% of the restaurant company stock was distributed to his daughter Elaine's husband, the favored Jimmy Slater and his family. Abe Wechsler kept no shares in Restaurant Associates, an interesting fact, since in later years he would take credit for the success of Restaurant Associates. Brody accepted Wechsler's proposal, which was not that generous an offer on Wechsler's part, since the restaurant stock was, on the surface, relatively worthless. Abe Wechsler had no confidence in the restaurant business; in Abe Wechsler's mind, the stock he had granted Brody was likely to remain worthless.

Brody's ability to vote the 52% of the restaurant company stock, however, would depend on his and Grace's identity of interests, and Grace and Jerry were living a married life in which their closeness and sympathy for one another were sadly lacking.

The Rikers stores were doing all right, and would do very well once Brody had managed a re-design of some of the key locations. Rikers stores were stocked from a central commissary, and the food was served up on an efficient conveyer belt system. Orders were given to the kitchen over a public address system. A re-design emulating the style of Piet Mondrian was very successful and Brody designed a couple of the other stores. During the War, most of the employees were women and labor relations were good. That would change with the return of the men and a hostile brand of unionism, but, early on, there was little trouble. With enough financing, it seemed that Rikers could evolve into a successful business.

But money was not available to make over enough of the other locations. Brody tried to raise $300,000 to do 10 additional Rikers, but could not. The Rikers' stockholders, Brody's in-laws, had no faith in the company. They were deaf to any long term approaches. When Brody sought financing from outside sources, inevitably the answer would be "Go to the coffee people; they're in the business of financing restaurants." And Brody discovered that Wechsler and his partners, after refusing financing to Rikers, had invested in the competition, helping to finance a Rudleys at 86th Street and Third Avenue. For Brody, that was an unforgivable insult.

One day, Brody, standing on the corner of 104th Street and Broadway, contemplated the new, efficient, and attractively designed Horn & Hardart. It had class and clout, and, seeing that, he felt that Rikers simply could not compete.

He needed new capital. He needed to grow in a different direction.

Port of New York Authority

At least Rikers had a small positive cash flow by then, even if it was plagued by insufficient capital to grow and change. Considering that when Brody had taken over as president, the company was on the edge of failure, his record of achievement was there for potential new backers to examine. But still, Brody was a young man with no experience in business other than having managed the Dartmouth College newspaper.

His Air Force service, however, was a definite plus. While his military résumé was irrelevant to his business colleagues, the self-confidence and straightforward can-do attitude that the military nurtured in him inspired confidence in his colleagues. That someone his age was able to find allies as highly placed and experienced as Brody did still seems remarkable. The essential credential Brody had was his own character and the impression he made.

Like many other successful executives, Brody's good size alone makes him seem impressive. His brown-blonde hair, sky blue eyes, and athletic build are attractive. On formal occasions such as Ascot or Longchamps, he is notably elegant. His smile is warm, and it is a relief to see its sudden emergence after one of his abrupt, even harsh, business assessments. What Brody's early backers must have seen and liked is what is still a hallmark of his business attitude: he believes that large and complex goals are achievable and his confidence is infectious. He has the master builder's large vision and the craftsman's belief that all you have to do to complete a grand task is to do the small tasks one at a time.

He is not at all arrogant. He is demanding, but implies no sense of superiority. Because it is always clear that he will tolerate neither sloth nor dishonesty, a healthy caution in dealing with him is advisable. He is uncomfortable with compliments and prefers his deeds to speak for themselves.

He and Grace both came from wealthy families. They felt at ease in New York, knew how to entertain, and how to be entertained. They expected to have access to influential people. That background was a helpful one, but Brody's business needs were urgent and no amiable networking was going to comfortably provide him with solutions to his complex business needs.

In order to grow with little capital, his first efforts were, and forever after that have been, to find extraordinary landlords who would finance restaurant installations for their own purposes. The first landlord with whom he made any headway was the Port of New York Authority.

Brody came to know and admire the head of its real estate department, Robert Curtiss and his assistant Bill Graham. After a series of discussions, they offered Restaurant Associates a 6-foot frankfurter stand in the old Newark Airport. The frankfurter stand had become available because the two partners who ran it became involved in a bitter, insoluble falling out. One of the partners was Sam Tieger, who owned a restaurant called the Tavern, in Newark, the other was Lou Rubin, who owned Rudleys in New York and also some "tablecloth" restaurants. It had devolved into the kind of battle where neither would let the other take over or be bought out, so they gave up the concession entirely.

In 1950, the Port Authority selected RA to run the stand; Brody immediately seized the opportunity by offering innovative features such as a 15-cent, foot-long frankfurter and establishing his own financial control system. The stand tripled in annual sales. No new personnel needed to be hired. To the Port Authority, who were entitled to a percentage of the take, Brody had done a great job. Brody had won the trust of Austin Tobin, the strong, dignified executive director, whose backing was key to all those seeking to do business with the Port Authority.

In 1953, the Port Authority awarded Brody other concessions at Newark Airport. Brody put the coffee shop under the management of Rikers stores. He opened a liquor bar, an employees' cafeteria, and a restaurant on the upper level of the airport terminal, the Newarker, which was to become RA's first venture into full-service, tablecloth dining.

Five months after taking over the operations of Rikers, Brody fired Henry Montagu, president of Rikers, and hired Austin Cox as director of personnel. Brody felt that choice of personnel would determine the future of his company. In 1983, when *National Restaurant News* devoted an issue to a Restaurant Associates retrospective, the lead headline was "Spawning Ground for Greatness." Brody was to do the job of talent selection better than anyone else in the industry before or since. But in 1953, in order to run The Newarker properly, he knew he had to go outside Restaurant Associates.

At the same time that Brody was developing the interests of RA at Newark Airport, he was seeking from the start-up New York State Thruway Authority the operations contract for the Corner House Restaurants the Authority would build, equip and pay for along the stretch of Thruway from Syracuse to Buffalo. To do business with such landlords was what Brody had decided was the future of RA.

In order to determine whether RA's qualifications would allow it to be an acceptable bidder, Brody went to the offices of Harris, Kerr, Foster, the famous hotel and restaurant auditors, who had been appointed food and beverage consultants to the Thruway Authority. There he met with Mike Warfel.

At lunch, Jerry told Warfel about the Newarker situation and asked him if he knew anybody at that level of management who could help him with the Newarker. Warfel told him of a former employee of theirs who was food and beverage manager of the Schine Hotels and was now based in Florida, but who wanted to return to New York. He was looking for a job. His name was Joe Baum. Brody sent for Baum, who came up to New York to be interviewed. Brody hired Baum to manage the Newarker.

Baum assumed his duties at the Newarker after the restaurant had been designed and constructed, and, therefore, missed the intense unpleasantness involved in its design. Baum's life-long penchant for taking credit for all aspects of a restaurant's success whether or not he had anything to do with it was given some early exercise at the Newarker, when he would take credit for the design and construction of the Newarker.

Brody had seen and admired the work of Herman Sachs, an architect with modest credentials, but with what to Brody were sound ideas. Brody persuaded the Port Authority to hire Sachs, and Sachs was grateful for the opportunity. But, with his hiring, a dramatic metamorphosis took place. Now seeing himself as working for the Port Authority and not for Brody, Sachs refused to show Brody the working drawings. Brody was infuriated and had to appeal to Robert Curtiss of the Port Authority to tell

Sachs that he had to refer everything to Brody for his approval. The work went ahead, and Brody prevailed, but nothing went easily or pleasantly.

Baum was now managing The Newarker, but things did not at first run smoothly. Baum had recruited Swiss chef, Albert Stockli, of the Claridge Hotel in Atlantic City. The team developed a continental menu, which was aimed at the people who lived in and around Newark Airport, but the restaurant attracted little business. Soon after the opening in 1953, Brody contacted a leading public relations firm in Newark and invited its chief executive for dinner at the Newarker.

Brody timed the meeting badly. The restaurant was empty, and the public relations man and Brody dined in splendid isolation. After analyzing the operation and its potential, this experienced public relations man showed an integrity rare to his profession when he refused to take Brody's account, because, he told Brody, it was hopeless. He could think of nothing that would stimulate trade.

Two weeks later, however, Brody found another public relations firm, which plunged into solving the problem. It was a one-man show run by Emanuel Denby, and he came up with a brilliant scheme.

The Newarker was using cutlery manufactured and distributed by the International Silver Company, and somehow or other, Denby persuaded International Silver to give the Newarker an award for that estimable choice. The award was presented at a press event by the head of the Gourmet Society, and the story broke in the local newspapers.

The day the story broke, Brody got a call from Robert Curtiss of the Port Authority, who congratulated him on the Gourmet award. From that moment on, The Newarker began to have status in the Newark community, which picked up momentum as customers, who discovered how good Baum and Stockli's menu and cooking were, spread the word.

Baum added his own unique brand of culinary showmanship. The Newarker became famous for its generous portions. Baum invented a presentation of Absecon oysters, called "knife and fork oysters" because they were so large they had to be eaten with a knife and fork. A seventh oyster, presented on its own plate, was added to the half dozen. A third claw was added to every order of lobster. Sparklers dazzled from the top of birthday cakes.

Soon people believed that dining at the Newarker was as good as dining in New York and that they could save themselves a bothersome trip. In fact, many of the customers of the Newarker invited their New York friends to come out to Newark. However, just as this enthusiastic support for the Newarker was getting underway, it was derailed by a ghastly series of airplane accidents in neighboring Elizabeth, New Jersey. Newark Airport was closed down for 5 months.

When the Newarker reopened, business was at first slow, but business overall was kept alive by revenue from the frankfurter stand, the coffee shop, liquor bar, and the employees' commissary. Business at the Newarker, did, at last, become re-established and quickly accelerated, until it became cash flow positive. Eventually gross sales of the Newarker reached $3 million and 90% of its customers were not airport travelers.

The Newarker had given RA more than a financially sound tablecloth restaurant. It had become a marshalling center for some of the best people RA would have working for it in the coming years, fulfilling Brody's belief that the success of his operations would depend on his personnel.

Early Newarker alumni include Joe Baum, who became one of the most influential and creative executives in the restaurant industry, working at the Forum of the Twelve Caesars, La Fonda del Sol, and the Four Seasons. Alan Lewis, Baum's right-hand man for a year and a half, later went to the Forum, where he helped Brody research Roman decor and dining habits in Pompeii and Naples. Stuart Levin, the back-of-the-house manager at the Newarker subsequently became the assistant director of the Forum when it opened in December 1958 and then manager of the Four Seasons. He also was manager of the Hawaiian Room, which Joe Baum and Albert Stockli used as a test kitchen for the Four Seasons. Tony Cabot, a Broadway conductor and musical director, started in 1955 and arranged the entertainment for every subsequent restaurant opening and special event. William Dickinson started as a waiter at the Newarker and eventually became captain at the Forum. Bryan Daly was a manager-trainee at the Newarker in 1958. After a stint as associate director of the Forum, he left in 1964 to join Brody and Fred Platzer, executive chef of the Newarker, in opening the Rainbow Room. Austin B. Cox became industrial relations director of RA and was responsible for hiring many of the people who composed the nucleus of the RA empire. His operation was crucial to the growth of RA, and the rapid growth of the RA restaurant empire would not have been possible without the staffing he had provided.

Now that RA had a successful tablecloth restaurant and not just a series of Rikers counters and institutional cafeterias, Brody could think of greater glory, the attempt at which resulted in the Hawaiian Room in the Hotel Lexington in New York. But before the reinvention of the Hawaiian Room under RA's management got under way, there was still the matter of the New York State Thruway and the Corner House restaurant concession.

The New York State Thruway

The Thruway Authority had divided the Thruway into three sections—New York to Albany, Albany to Syracuse, and Syracuse to Buffalo and produced a set of drawings of what the typical restaurant would look like. The restaurant operators were given no design input. Executive director Holden Evans scheduled a meeting of the bidders in Albany.

Brody was there along with William Marriott (the original Bill Marriott), Howard Johnson (the original Howard Johnson) and two executives of the enormously powerful Union News Company. For RA to undertake the management of a section of the New York State Thruway's concessions was ambitious, even though, financially, the only requirement would be having enough working capital.

Brody did his homework well and, in the course of the meeting with Evans, asked many questions. In fact, Brody's questions dominated the meeting, and, finally Evans turned to the other potential bidders and said, "Doesn't anybody else have any questions?" At which point, Howard Johnson said, "He's doing all right." For Brody and Johnson that was the beginning of a friendship, which lasted through the remainder of Johnson's life.

That his competitors were so amiable did not surprise Brody. Any successful bidder would encounter the same problems as any other; therefore, all were well-served by the thoroughness of Brody's vetting. The meeting may have been competitive but it was not at all acrimonious.

Because the restaurant operators had been given no say in the design of the restaurants, in the following days, Brody tried to come up with an idea to make the RA plan special. Shortly after the meeting with Evans, Brody made an appointment with a member of the Thruway Authority, a partner in the law firm of former New York Governor Thomas Dewey. Brody floated the notion that the New York State Thruway become the "gourmet highway." Operators would be allowed to serve a distinctive kind of food, such as seafood, or an ethnic variety such as German or Irish, so that in the Syracuse to Buffalo stretch of the Thruway, there might be as many as 15 kinds of menu types, giving representation to New York State's diversity. Brody's idea was met with stunned silence.

Nonetheless, RA entered the bidding process. As previously mentioned, all RA needed was working capital, and, at this point, RA had a going business—small, but vital—and a restaurant with a good name.

If a restaurant is to be a success from its inception, it develops working capital by taking in revenue before it has to pay bills or indeed payroll. The Newarker, however, was not enjoying such an ideal start, but it demonstrated that Brody's team was competent and promising. The Thruway Authority had anticipated that the Thruway restaurants had a captive audience and the carefully prepared automotive and restaurant traffic projections its consultants had produced indicated that each restaurant would immediately be self-financing. The Thruway Authority awarded the Syracuse to Buffalo franchise to RA. Brody had confidence in these projections.

Brody assigned his director of purchasing, Harold Simpson, to work around the clock to upgrade the restaurants, yet, even so, the initial euphoria of the victory was soon replaced by worry. The Thruway took longer than expected to build up traffic. Panic took hold of Brody's in-laws when the Thruway did not open to sufficiently large crowds of people and automobiles.

Despite the monumental effort it had taken to open each restaurant, after a year and a half, Wechsler and his stockholders sold their section of the Thruway to Gladieux Foods of Ohio for a modest profit. Time and patience would have made the concession worth millions.

Except in the eyes of his in-laws and his own wife who was voting 42% of RA's stock, Brody's victory was validation of his long-term financial strategy and, for most of the restaurant community, further evidence of his credibility as an executive with vision and daring.

The Hawaiian Room &
The Forum of the
Twelve Caesars

The Hawaiian Room was a theme restaurant located in the Lexington Hotel on Lexington Avenue and East 48th Street in New York City. It had enjoyed many years of success, but was in the doldrums. Its owner and the owner of the Lexington Hotel, Saul Hertzig, a friend of Brody's, whispered to him at a cocktail party that he was going to close the restaurant. Hertzig knew something of Brody's appetite for expansion; his story was not without strategic intent. Brody was definitely interested.

Hertzig's strengths, along with his predicaments, made him just the kind of landlord for whom Brody was looking. Hertzig viewed the returant's potential discouragingly and would, therefore, offer an attractive deal. There would be minimal start-up costs, because the Hawaiian Room was already in business, and renovations would be the landlord's responsibility. Brody signed a modest lease.

Brody appointed Joe Baum corporate vice president responsible for the operation of the Hawaiian Room and Austin Cox chief of personnel. The Hawaiian Room became a great success, largely due to a strategy, which Brody perfected in other successful ventures. The theme had to be validated by more than just decor. Brody went to Hawaii in order to research the cuisine, decor, and dining styles and then sent the management team there. For Joe Baum, who had never been to Hawaii or to Europe, these culinary research junkets were an important part of his education.

Philip Miles, RA's vice-president in charge of public relations, who headed up publicity for the Hawaiian Room remembered, "researching the hell out of each new restaurant, with executives scouring Europe, Central America, and Mexico to obtain the exact feel of each place. They visited every major kitchen in France and England....RA enhanced the education of the American palate and raised all the standards dramatically."

The operation of the Hawaiian Room was blessed with several major publicity events. Arthur Godfrey one of America's most popular television personalities, was key. The Hawaiian entertainer, Holly Loki, who strummed her ukulele and swayed her sarong-draped hips, regularly appeared on Godfrey's Number One ranked TV show. Godfrey often joined in on his own ukulele.

Godfrey was a regular guest at the Lexington Hotel and always ordered his dinner from room service. One night Brody took the risk of substituting food prepared by the Hawaiian Room for Godfrey's room service order. Godfrey loved it and decided to feature a luau from the Hawaiian Room on his TV show. The event was so successful that Steve Allen, another leading TV host, decided to do the same thing. These two shows appeared about two weeks apart on national network television. The impact was tremendous.

An even greater coup was to follow. Brody wanted to arrange a by-invitation-only, world-class celebrity party—the kind of party which reached its ultimate perfection with Truman Capote's "Black and White Ball"—at the Hawaiian Room. Brody and

Philip Miles were friends of Morton Gottlieb, a Broadway stage manager on his way to becoming a producer, and put Gottlieb in charge of bringing in the "Beautiful People." Miles used his influence to get LIFE Magazine to cover the party, which they agreed to do if LIFE were the only press permitted.

The host and hostess were Richard and Sibyl Burton, and the party consisted of every leading player on Broadway. All the celebrities ate on the floor, luau-style, provided with exotic tropical drinks. The women wore sarongs and little else. Brody put a large children's swimming pool with a water slide in the dining room. Lawrence Olivier's lady companion zipped down the slide to earn the coconut drink and funny hat you got at the bottom. She claimed she had hurt her back and sued, but not before madly dancing the night away. Maureen Stapleton caroused with the Puerto Rican chief of maintenance for the restaurant, who perhaps in the intensity of the occasion, she mistook for one of the thespians.

The accumulation of publicity was so dramatic that Tony Cabot, who arranged music and entertainment for the Hawaiian Room, informed Brody that Gus Eyssell, president of Rockefeller Center and the real estate executive in charge of attracting new clients, was interested in meeting Brody.

Eyssell offered Brody a space which was actually the delivery entrance to the Rockefeller Center theater. RA's presence there would end The Union News Company's monopoly of all the restaurants in Rockefeller Center, including the Rainbow Room.

Brody and Eyssell worked out a lease, but Rockefeller Center was a less pliant landlord than Brody would ideally have liked. Try as he might, Brody could get Rockefeller Center to construct only the basic structure of the new restaurant, bringing the utilities to the point of hookup, but no further. The rest of the installations, costing $500,000, would have to be done with RA's own capital, and, at that price, Brody would have to borrow a significant portion .

To make sure that the project was feasible, Brody had consulted with his design architects throughout the course of the lease negotiations. But when the moment of truth was at hand—to sign or not to sign—Brody felt that they still had not created an arresting enough interior design concept. In the next two days Brody scheduled meetings with various interior decorators and, finally, fixed on William Pahlmann.

Pahlmann showed Brody twelve Roman imperial portraits, which Pahlmann owned, and which stood in storage in an art warehouse. Pahlmann suggested using them in the restaurant. Brody could not imagine buying the entire dozen, but Pahlmann pointed out that just one or two would have no effect: "They were a complete set." Brody bought the dozen for $500 each and, from there, it wasn't far to the "Forum of the Twelve Caesars."

Philip Miles had been given the job of making sure the new restaurant had what *new* restaurants appropriately find it difficult to claim: tradition. At a time when even the name of the restaurant had not yet been chosen, Miles felt somewhat dazed by the challenge.

Eventually, after the job of imperial artifice was completed, Miles issued a five page, single-spaced document to all employees of the Forum, explaining the spirit and the *raison d'être* of the restaurant. "The Romans of that golden age knew how to live well and how to dine well....We have tried to be faithful to the spirit of Roman elegance, but in a contemporary manner."

As they had at the Hawaiian Room, Brody and his team began the research necessary to create an authentically historic dining experience. In the course of their travels they made trips to the Museum of Roman Civilization in Rome, the Museum of Pompeii, the National Museum in Naples, the Kaiser Friedrich

Museum in Berlin and the British Museum in London. In the library of Cornell University, they found a rare manuscript detailing the cookery of imperial Rome. In a test kitchen of glass, aluminum, and stainless steel, the Epicurean treasures of the ancients went on trial.

A leading design magazine described the Forum of the Twelve Casears with gusto:

> The foyer mirror began life as a Regency doorway and the statues on each side of it are out of the first Napoleonic Empire....The dozen busts of the Caesars at the bar, romantic relics of Europe in the 1880s, were purchased from an estate being broken up in Easthampton, Long Island. The candelabrum on the main column in the dining room is antique French with panels of gold-leafed, carved wood. Where the cocktail tables are not of mosaic marble, they are of inlaid woods, principally ebony and mahogany. The Bacchus head in the bar is bronze crafted in Milan; another, elsewhere, is of marble quarried in Rome. The bar and entrance are paneled in cherry; the walls of the dining room covered in red Italian Fortuny; the wall banquettes are in dark-brown leather and the tables in the center of the room in beige leather tooled in gold.
>
> A huge mosaic purporting to show life in Rome is on the east wall of the bar. In the dining room itself, surveying all with airs suitable to their temperaments, are large portraits of the Caesars....

Brody and Baum, in consultation with experts and friends, such as Geraldine Hotchner and the sculptor Beverly Pepper, who had toured Brody through the sites of ancient Rome, fashioned a wondrous menu. The food and restaurant columnist, Julia Edwards, having dined at The Forum, wrote,

From prologue to epilogue, from the bowl of olives, looking like multi-colored grapes, to the last flaming frivolity, the Crepes of the Mad Nero, the magnificent menu casts such a spell of opulence that one is likely to find himself ordering the Pheasant of the Golden House on a Silver Shield in Gilded Plumage or Truffle Stuffed Quail, Cleopatra—Wrapped in Macedonian Vine Leaves, Baked in Hot Ashes.

After dining at the Forum, Secretary of State John Foster Dulles sent this letter to the ailing General Walter Bedell Smith: "Dear Beedle," wrote Dulles, "When in New York last week at the United Nations...we went to the Forum. We were well received and fed to great satisfaction. Toward the end of the dinner, the manager told me that you were a member of the Board of Directors, which own the restaurant. It is my recommendation that instead of going to hospitals to get intravenous injections and the like, you should visit more frequently this excellent restaurant of yours. I am sure it would be much more fun."

But as much fun as the Forum was, it was expensive fun. The Forum had cost RA $500,000 and had to conform to Brody's economic principles. In leaving the world of Rikers behind, Brody had made a decision based on his view of the near- and middle-term American economy. Brody told Gilbert Millstein of *Esquire*, "This country within the foreseeable future is scheduled for a period of full employment, creeping inflation and fairly uninterrupted prosperity. When you have that kind of economy, there are profits to be made in consumer industries that do not involve necessities." As he said when he "was pushed into Rikers in 1947, we had a $135,000 overdraft and a large inventory we didn't need. We've still got a big overdraft, but there are a couple of basic differences: then we had an all-cash operation and that was it; today we have very substantial accounts receivable."

As long as the economy aligned itself to Brody's prophecy, the creativity and hard work of his and his staff would prevail. For now, all was blue skies and clear sailing.

Even as Brody was developing the design of the Forum of the Twelve Caesars, he began the quest for what would become the Four Seasons. The Wechslers would take no part, just as they had taken no part in the development of the Hawaiian Room and the Forum. They seemed content to know nothing, and that was more than all right with Brody. As for Brody's wife Grace, she didn't care either.

On the infrequent occasions the Wechslers did place themselves into the action, they invariably undercut Brody's efforts. Six months after beginning the design for the Forum, Brody found a location for a new Rikers store on 42nd Street, relatively near the Daily News Building. It appeared to be a 24-hour operation and it was available at a rent Brody thought RA could afford. When Brody discussed the matter with his in-laws, at first they thought it was a good idea and then they became critical of it. Eventually, Brody discovered that the location was taken over by an outsider with financing from the Wechslers. It was a reprise of the Rudley betrayal. This was the last time Brody ever told his in-laws about any pending project, including the Four Seasons.

The Four Seasons

Grace had as little interest in Brody's life as a restaurant executive as her father had. Her life revolved around her golf, her art and sculpture, and her social life. She made a point of not dining in any restaurant in which Brody had an interest, not even the ones he had designed.

But Brody's intense focus on his restaurant activities was not at all deterred by his wife's distance from them. Brody's social life more and more centered on his daytime meetings and luncheons with his brilliant and ever more celebrated RA team. And while the restaurants were not generating significant profit, they were generating enough cash flow to allow Brody and Grace to live comfortably. The children remained unaware of their parents' misalliance. The family usually ate diner together, and the kids adored their father and thought that he was above all fun to be with. When the divorce came, all of the children would be taken totally by surprise.

If Grace and Brody had shared any mutual interests, they could have afforded to indulge them, but they had no shared interests. Their very lack of a relationship gave free space for the expansion of Brody's life as a restaurant industry workaholic.

Brody and his expanding Restaurant Associates empire were attracting the attention of the financial, architectural, and culinary worlds. None of it interested Grace.

When Grace suggested that the family move to suburbia, Brody was glad to oblige because of the existence of excellent school systems for the children. Scarsdale was chosen because the experts at the Fieldston School praised its public school system. The possibility that suburban life would entangle him and Grace in a tighter world of suburban society and give them less space to keep their distance from one another did not alarm Brody. His attention was, for the most part, elsewhere.

In the 1950s, there was no more prestigious address in America than New York's Park Avenue. From Grand Central Station north to 96th Street, New York society lived in clubby awareness of their privilege, occupying high-rise, pre-war apartment coops, often with ten or more rooms, guarded by white-gloved doormen in formal livery. South of 57th Street the residential nature of Park Avenue was giving way to big business towers, sheeted in plate glass, designed by the leading architects of the world. Lever House was the first of the steel and glass monuments to capitalism's aspirations and would soon become its most admired architectural achievement. In 1958, there was to be a rival to the beauty of Lever House. Seagram would put up its skyscraper headquarters on the east side of Park Avenue, between 52nd and 53rd Streets.

Seagram had cooperated with the City Zoning Board by providing a large setback from Park Avenue. The ensuing space provided a generous perspective from which to view the powerfully elegant façade of copper-colored steel and reflective plate glass.

Midtown office workers, executives, and tourists could sun themselves during the lunch hours, mellowing out to the white noise of the two Mies Van der Rohe designed pools and fountains, which adorned the north and south ends of the Park Avenue esplanade. Even before construction was completed, businesses competed for space, wanting to partake in the clout that the Seagram Building bestowed on its residents.

Seagram chief, Sam Bronfman, had decided to donate the space that would become the Four Seasons for the use of charities in need of an elegant and visible venue for their fundraisers. Sam's son, Edgar, fearing that the competition among charities to secure the favored venue would mire Seagram in inter-charity squabbles and time-consuming diplomacy, managed to get the charity plan shelved and to substitute for it the search for a superb restaurateur. Henri Soulé, Bronfman's first choice, was too occupied with Le Pavillion to consider another major undertaking.

Edgar Bronfman and Brody had talked business and exchanged pleasantries whenever Bronfman had dined at the Forum of the Twelve Caesars. Bronfman was impressed by Brody's ambition to raise the stature of Restaurant Associates, which he knew had its roots in the coffee business and in Rikers Cafeterias. Bronfman judged that RA's rise to its current renown was all the more impressive on account of the distance traveled upwards.

Bronfman was also of the impression that RA was in rock-solid financial shape, an impression gleaned mainly by the celebrity of Brody's accomplishments, which, unknown to Bronfman, had been achieved on a tenuously resilient shoestring.

Not only to Edgar Bronfman, but to the world-at-large, Jerry Brody's RA financial *bona fides* were in order. In fact they were precarious, the viability of the entire enterprise largely dependent on Brody's carefully balancing day-to-day income against bills due.

While the Seagram Building was still a hole in the ground, Brody dreamed of having a restaurant there. The name on the construction fence told Brody that the real estate broker was Cushman and Wakefield. Brody arranged a meeting with its chairman, L'Huillier Shaef, and told him of his desire to establish a restaurant on the plaza level. The news was music to Shaef's ears; the plan to use the ground floor for charity meeting spaces would generate no retail revenue for Cushman and Wakefield. When Shaef heard glowing reports from the Port Authority about Brody, he was further persuaded to recommend RA for the proposed restaurant space.

Six months later, Shaef arranged a luncheon for Brody with Phyllis Lambert, who after her recent divorce had just been appointed project manager of the Seagram Building by her father, Sam Bronfman, and had been instrumental in getting Mies van der Rohe to be its architect.

Knowing how important it was to impress Lambert favorably, Brody hired a limousine and drove her out to Newark Airport for lunch. It was not the most opulent choice, but Brody was honestly proud of the transformation of the Newarker.

Lambert ate her lunch in silence, making no comments whatsoever on what Brody was saying. If she had formed an opinion, she did not offer it. Brody delivered her back to her office and reported the gist of the meeting to Shaef, assuming that Lambert's non-reaction to his proposal was the end of the project.

Six months went by and then Shaef arranged another luncheon meeting for Brody, this time with Edgar Bronfman, who had just been named president of Seagram. Edgar Bronfman and Brody had met before, and on one of those occasions, Bronfman told Brody that he had formed some unkind impressions of Abe Wechsler's business practices. Bronfman asked Brody if he knew anything about some of Wechsler's alleged business improprieties. Brody said that he did not. It is ironic that years later, after Brody's ouster from RA, Wechsler, wherever he traveled, was proud to bill himself as the force behind the Four Seasons-Seagram deal. In fact, he was never introduced into any of those meetings nor into the meetings in regard to the public offering.

Brody hosted Bronfman at lunch in a nearby hotel, the Kings Inn, with a redone dining room, which Brody had never been in before, but which he had assumed would be basic, plastic and ordinary. If Brody did not want to make business take a back seat to dining and decor, he could have hardly chosen better. Bronfman brought along his chief financial officer, Sidney Fried, and this time the reaction to Brody's proposal was businesslike, specific and encouraging. Because Brody knew that Seagram had, by that time, talked with other restaurateurs, he was particularly pleased by Bronfman's encouragement.

Shaef called Brody the next day and told him that in a few days, a Friday, he was to meet with Sam Bronfman at the Seagram Building. Promptly, just before 5:00 PM, Brody arrived at Edgar Bronfman's office and found Sidney Fried. The two men sat down at a small director's table, with Brody at the head and Fried alongside. When the doors opened, in came 80-year old Mr. Sam on the arm of Edgar, and they sat with Edgar next to Fried, and Sam opposite. Thirty-five year old Brody found himself at the head of the table. Brody felt quite comfortable, and, after a little bit of small talk, Mr. Sam said, "I understand you want to do a restaurant in our building."

Brody took that as his cue and launched into all the reasons he could think of why there should be a fine dining restaurant in their building. Brody said that the building was their home and that they were in a hospitality-related business. They should be seen as welcoming people into their home and develop an environment that was appropriate to their products. By now, having made the presentation for the third time. Brody felt he was at least well- rehearsed.

Mr. Sam settled more and more deeply into his chair, getting more and more comfortable, until he dozed off, despite the fact that Brody talked louder and louder. Brody had been a year getting to this point. Finally he was in front of the key person, but apparently one who found Brody's proposition so unengaging that it induced sleep.

Edgar, who had been paying keen attention, asked Brody a helpful question, and turned to see if his father had heard it. He then reached for a pencil, and, in cadence with the question, which he repeated, rapped on the table and Mr. Sam woke up. And that was it. Mr. Sam said, "All right, I think we'll proceed. We'll have our man contact you." Brody, feeling pretty chipper by then, said, "Well you can have your man contact my man." The meeting ended.

From that point on Brody negotiated the lease with Seagram's in-house counsel, who, in the grand scheme of things, considered Brody's project of no great importance. Brody depended upon his own lawyers very little, passing drafts in front of them and getting suggestions, but essentially conducting negotiations alone.

The proceedings were hardly adversarial. Seagram wanted RA's expertise, and, after all, they were funding the entire operation and knew for certain that they needed to because it was certainly beyond RA's financial capabilities. RA agreed to pay Seagram a rent amounting to a modest percentage of the gross plus an additional 2% towards retiring Seagram's investment. In addition to the generosity of the financial arrangement, RA was given design control. Brody believes that the Seagram house counsel had never dealt with such an issue and thus was willing to be relieved of the problem by putting it into Brody's hands. After all, the lawyers knew Brody had received the full blessing of Mr. Sam.

Once the lease was finished, Brody made up a list of proposed designers with whom he would like to work. He took his list to Philip Johnson and asked him for a recommendation. Johnson was shocked and said, "Well, what about me?" Brody tried hard to control his eagerness. Not only was Seagram picking up the entire fee for the designers, but also Johnson was Brody's covert first choice. Johnson organized a show at the famous "Glass House" in Darien, Connecticut, and did his best to convince Brody to use him, which was not at all difficult.

And so Phyllis Lambert, Brody and Johnson started the task of designing the Four Seasons and also the Brasserie with which the Bronfmans had decided to complement the Four Seasons. The restaurants had to fit into spaces that had not been planned for them. Brody and his team met in Johnson's office every Wednesday for about two years, along with Phyllis Lambert, the same woman who had shown no interest in Brody's plans when he took her to lunch at the Newarker.

Lambert was the project manager of the entire Seagram building, including the restaurant. Everything was her business and, sometimes Brody's suggestions horrified her. But Brody, not Lambert, had veto power, despite the fact that it was all Seagram money.

Plans for development of the restaurant began in earnest and top-level design considerations were discussed in detail. Only Lambert was there to speak for Seagram. Crucial design elements led to disagreements. For example, at first, Mies van der Rohe refused to pierce the podium that the building stood on; all entrances would have had to be through the lobby. By piercing the podium, entrances on the side streets could be created, allowing for better traffic flow, more interesting design opportunities, and less dissipation in the overall design, for fire exits, deliveries, and refuse removal. On these fundamental matters Brody and Johnson got their way.

Then the design battle turned to interior decor. Brody wanted to create a "New York" restaurant, not knowing exactly what that would entail. He knew that if he could establish such a restaurant, one that would be a peer of the great European dining showcases, that it could spearhead a new era in American fine dining.

Brody's wishes did not deter Phyllis Lambert from pursuing her passion for a Picasso-driven motif for the new restaurant. At one point, the Seagram treasurer implied that Seagram would buy anything that the restaurant wanted, as long as it was an original Picasso. They wanted Brody to name the restaurant The Picasso. As an investment strategy, Brody understood the reasoning behind acquiring important Picassos and then increasing their value by showcasing them in a great restaurant.

A huge 20' x 22' painted curtain, which Picasso executed in 1919 for the Diaghilev and Massine Ballet "Le Tricorne" was for sale at the Perls Gallery. It was too tall for the Museum of Modern Art, but not, thought Lambert, for the Four Seasons. But, as much as Lambert wanted the Picasso curtain to hang in the nave of the restaurant, she knew that she had to come to Brody for approval. Brody said, "I like it, but not here." At which point, Lambert stormed out. Brody relented, making a wise decision, both politically and aesthetically, when he accepted the Picasso curtain. He did not, however, hang it in the nave where he felt it would dominate the main dining room, defining the decor by overpowering everything else. Instead it was hung between the pool and grillrooms, where it is still admired by Picasso lovers.

Lambert's Picasso-philia did not go away, and Brody called in allies to bolster his resistance. Brody hired William Pahlmann, his interior designer for the Forum. Pahlmann's man, George Thiele, conceived of the notion of a pool in the middle of the north dining room, and, in his drawings, he demonstrated that there would be no loss of seating space. Philip Johnson embraced the idea, but he and Lambert wanted to adorn the pool with a series of bronze easels executed by Picasso called "The Bathers." Brody eager to show that he would spare no time and expense to demonstrate his fair-handedness, traveled to Paris to see "The Bathers," but decided that they would be ugly in that space. He rejected them.

The last time the Picasso battle was fought was in conjunction with lighting in the bar room area. LIFE Magazine had featured a series of John Milos's slow-exposure photographs of Picasso's whirling a flashlight, creating fantastic shapes. Johnson brought these photographs to one of their meetings and announced at a subsequent one that they had inspired his solution to lighting the barroom. Picasso would bend neon tubes and they would be placed at the tops of the walls as illuminated moldings. Brody said, "I think that would be terrible."

Philip Johnson, who was invariably charming, patient, and above all, professional, was goaded into losing his temper. He committed the tactical error of exclaiming at Brody "Well, if you don't want that, what do you want?" Brody knew.

"What about something by that fellow who did the small sculpture in the Metropolitan Museum called 'The Sun': Richard Lippold?" Johnson further eroded his authority by asking "Who?" Brody repeated the name and elaborated on his evaluation of Lippold. The meeting came to a close with the hiring of Lippold. When Johnson went to see Lippold's work, he was filled with admiration, and was fair enough to say so. And with that episode, the Picasso campaign came to an end.

Brody and Johnson went through every detail of the restaurant decor, even the appointments in the toilets. Johnson had placed a Brno chair in his office that had been done by Mies van der Rohe. Whenever Brody came into Johnson's office he would turn from what he was doing and look at it. Johnson told Brody that it was a chair that Mies had designed for the World's Fair in Czechoslovakia, but Brody would not be intimidated by its ancestry and eventually agreed with Johnson that the chairs were perfect for the Four Seasons. The two men confronted each other over almost every detail, but the confrontations led to better results.

The aspect of decor that presented the hardest challenge was the window coverings. The restaurant had 60' ceilings in a site with no view. With curtains in mind, Johnson hired Marie Nichols, a fabric designer. Brody got a call from Johnson to meet him in what was to be the pool dining room. It was still empty. No construction had begun. On one small section of window, Johnson had hung chain metal swags, resembling chainmail armor. They were perfect for the room, a real coup. Brody was thrilled. The two men hugged.

But the metal swags waved. Johnson told Brody that he would see that the waves were removed. However, Johnson discovered that the waves were caused by the difference in temperature between the side closest to the window and the side closest to the interior. Moreover, as the temperature equation shifted, the waves in the swags moved either up or down, adding more interest to the design. The swags remained and became one of the hallmarks of the Four Seasons.

Philip Johnson remained good-humored about Brody throughout the building of the Four Seasons and after. "It was said of me by Jerry," he remarked, "that I'm a son-of-a-bitch to

work with, but that once the thing was do
I am returning the compliment. The things
designs were worth vetoing, for one thing...
as a feeling-out thing, as many artists do, a

The Four Seasons achieved the imprin
of Modern Art, which included the Four Seasons ... ...
series of membership visits to noteworthy private collections.
Eighteen of the accouterments designed for the restaurant by
the team of Garth and Ada Louise Huxtable were added to its
permanent good design collection.

The job of constructing, designing, and preparing the restaurant for its first customers had taken $4.5 million and two long
years to complete. Today the job would cost upwards of $45
million.

Lambert and Johnson commissioned Mark Rothko, one of
the reigning artist of the New York School, to create a series of
canvases which would dominate the private dining room over-
looking the poolroom. As opening day in July 1959 approached,
Rothko refused to deliver. The reasons for Rothko's refusal are
still debated, but Rothko, who hated the rich, described the Four
Seasons to a friend of his as "a place where the richest bastards in
New York come to feed and show off. I accepted the assignment
as a challenge, with strictly malicious intentions. I hope to paint
something that will ruin the appetite of every son of a bitch who
ever eats in that room." It is not surprising that when Brody
invited him and his wife to dinner in order to solve the problem,
Rothko accepted the invitation and remained totally silent
throughout the meal. Years later, at his own studio at 222 The
Bowery, Rothko, using the dimensions of the rooms in the Four
Seasons as guidelines, completed the paintings he would have
done for the Four Seasons.

Brody needed to find appropriate art for the opening of the

rant. He contacted his friend from Ethical Culture days, the art collector, Ben Heller. With Heller in the lead, Brody ran around to all the galleries who offered works by New York School artists. Brody did not see one painting which he wanted to hang in the private dining room. At one point, the two men took a break and returned to Heller's apartment, where hanging on one of the walls was a very large Jackson Pollack painting entitled "Blue Poles." Brody loved it. He asked Heller if he would lend it to him. Heller agreed in return for Brody's making a contribution to his favorite charity.

Brody thought it was dazzling; the waiters, however, did not like it at all. They thought it looked like spilled food. They protested that they could not look at it. Brody let it hang (eventually "Blue Poles" was sold to an Australian collector for $2 million). Finally, through Philip Johnson, the Museum of Modern Art lent Brody a small sculpture by the French sculptor, Jean Arp, which was placed at the entranceway. Opening day arrived.

Just before the doors were to open to the public, Brody had a visit from Mrs. Sam Bronfman, who had never seen the space before. Brody gave her a tour. She was extremely complimentary and said, "May I bring Sam down?" Sam would never have ventured into the space uninvited.

About 5 PM, Mrs. Bronfman appeared at the Four Seasons with Sam, and Brody conducted another tour, and again Mrs. Bronfman was very complimentary. Sam said a few nice things, and as the party left, Brody turned to thank them both for their compliments. Mrs. Bronfman turned to Brody and said, "Thank *you* very much."

It was Joe Baum who proposed the name "the Four Seasons." It referred to the four weather seasons of New York and also its social seasons. It also gave the kitchen an opportunity to prepare four seasonal menus, which were complemented by seasonal changes in the decorations and the uniforms of the staff.

Brody had hired the great chef and gourmet, James Beard, to be a consultant to the restaurant. Brody, Joe Baum, and Chef Albert Stockli had worked hard to present a truly elegant, New York menu. Only a short time after the restaurant opening, Beard told Brody that his good friend, Craig Claiborne, was going to give the Four Seasons a poor review. Claiborne did not like the menu.

A man of less self-assurance than Brody would have been badly shocked by the damage such a review could do and resigned himself to the outcome. Instead, Brody asked Beard if he would arrange a luncheon at the Four Seasons with Craig Claiborne. Beard conveyed Brody's invitation and the gentlemanly Claiborne agreed.

Brody's defense at the luncheon was to take the offense. Accusing Claiborne of being a Francophile, Brody told him that he had never written a flattering review of an Italian or a Chinese restaurant, or, for that matter, any ethnic New York restaurant other than a French one. Rather than being offended or defensive, Claiborne took Brody's criticism as a fair comment. And, in that vein, he re-examined what the Four Seasons was trying to do. Claiborne gave the restaurant a positive review, but one which depressed the entire crew: "On the whole the cuisine is not exquisite in the sense that *la grande cuisine Française* at its superlative best is exquisite." That the food was not intended to be *la grande cuisine Française* was exactly what Brody had told Claiborne earlier when he had accused Claiborne of Gaelic ancestor worship. Fortunately the public was not deterred.

The opening of the Four Seasons was big news. It got a front-page story in the *New York Times*, which was more concerned with the construction costs of the restaurant than with anything else. In booming, post-World War II New York, there was nothing to match the expensive radiance of the Four Seasons. New Yorkers and Americans in general were giddy with the smell of newly-minted money. The opening of the Four Seasons was an event that had interest beyond the restaurant world. It was a sign, as was Lincoln Center, of the re-building of New York and of the emergence of New York not only as the economic capital of the world, but also as an embodiment of America's newly-born cultural self-assurance, perhaps, even, arrogance.

In order to keep the Four Seasons in the limelight, in 1962, Brody hired Earl Blackwell. As Roger Martin, a former public relations assistant director of Restaurant Associates said of the Four Seasons, "it was beautiful, cost millions of dollars, and had great food. But it was very *nouveau*. We weren't getting through to the people we wanted." Brody could not have hired an instrument more specifically designed for the purpose of attracting a more celebrated socially-annointed crowd of big spenders to the Four Seasons than Blackwell (known as "Mr. Celebrity"). He would later use Blackwell to promote the Rainbow Room and Raffles. A seat at the Four Seasons came to bestow power—all you had to do was believe it and with the help of Earl Blackwell, a lot of customers did.

In the 1950s, Blackwell had teamed up with Cleveland Amory to produce the first version of the *Celebrity Register*, a book of 2,240 biographies of famous people. A nod from Blackwell gratified even the rich and famous even though the book radiated Amory's irreverence and disdain. Blackwell, if he shared any of Amory's disdain, did not show it. He seemed to adore his clientele.

At the Four Seasons, according to Martin, Blackwell's job was "to direct his following, his coterie of people, to and through

Young Brody at Far Rockaway Beach with his sister Ellie and his father Jac.

Brody and Ellie flank their father Jac.

Brody's senior class picture at Ethical Culture School, where he told the awesome headmaster, Algernon Black, that it was his ambition to be a millionaire.

Brody, who left Dartmouth in his sophomore year to join the Air Force, in training at Greenville, Mississippi.

Brody with infant daughter Ricki born in Albuquerque, New Mexico.

The Four Seasons hosted a fund-raising dinner for Democratic donors before President Kennedy's 1963 birthday party at Madison Square Garden. Kennedy was driven himself to the restaurant in an open convertible, where he was greeted at curbside by Brody.

Marlene Gray, animal lover.
The future Mrs. Brody, at the
family tea plantation in Ceylon.

Marlene, just graduated from
the Ecole d'Interprètes of the
University of Geneva, and fluent
in German, Spanish, Italian, French
and English, accepted John
Steinbeck's offer to be his secretary
during his stay in Paris, 1954. Here
they walk in the Bois de Bologne.

Gallagher's Farm in Ghent, New York, has grown from 100 acres to over 600.
It is the home of Gallagher's Stud.

Brody and Manhattan Gal, who defeated Black Marshall or "Sporty," to become
Grand Champion of the Futurity at Louisville. She was only the third heifer to
become Grand Champion in 30 years, a feat roughly equal to a filly winning the
Triple Crown. (Wagner International Photos)

The Brodys about to receive the trophy awarded Patriot at the 1977 Western National Stock show in Denver for Grand Champion Bull. (Scott Brody photo)

Patriot, Grand Champion Bull, Western National Stock Show, 1977. (Scott Brody photo)

Gallagher's Farm

Thoroughbred Horses
Registered Aberdeen Angus

Ghent, New York 12075
518 392 4110

Marlene Brody

Jerome Brody

Dear Friends,

We are pleased to invite you to our "Family Affair" Sale. The cattle we are presenting have all been produced on our farm. They are all products of our breeding program.

That program began with the foundation females Manhattan Gal and Hedgerow's Jestress in 1976. Their progeny have achieved extraordinary showring success and have made major contributions to Angus breeding in this country. Symbolizing the maturity of our herd is a brand new show barn and sale facility where we shall welcome you.

We have deliberately kept our herd small. Genetics being the mystery that it is, even in ova transplant there are breeding disappointments. We cull those animals. We are not in the business of having a sale of culls. Included in the sale group are Calf Champion and Grand Champion Female at the Dutchess County Fair, Grand and Reserve Champion Females at the New York State Fair and at the Connecticut State Fair.

Many of the cows in the sale are in calf to **New Yorker**, the Grand Champion and Supreme Champion Bull at the 1984 All American Breeders Futurity.

Phil and Annie Trowbridge have contributed immeasureably to the success of our herd. Phil has been responsible for all the matings, as well as the entire general management of our farm. He has been very ably assisted by Mallory Mort with Jerry McCammon and Signe Egvar acting as our herdsman as well as Michael O'Neil who is a new member of the team at the farm. They have developed our farming program and the farm itself into a real showplace. We are grateful for their efforts.

We take real pride in the Angus we have produced, particularly for this sale, and are confident of their future success.

We look forward to seeing you on the weekend of October 19 and guarantee a great dinner on the evening of the 20th.

Sincerely,

Jerry Brody

Phil Trowbridge

Jerome Brody
Phil Trowbridge

Invitation to the 1984 Angus Dispersal Sale. Named "A Family Affair," the sale of the Gallagher's Stud herd brought in record prices and marked the end of Brody's brief and triumphant career as an Angus Breeder.

Phil Trowbridge and family. Counter-clockwise from bottom: wife Ann, Phil, and the children, P.J. and Amy.

Marlene, Brody and Ira Boggs at the Western National Stock Show, 1977. Boggs recommended that Brody purchase the heifer who became national champion Manhattan Gal.

the Four Seasons. He brought in whoever the names were. It was to …give it the stamp of approval with the people who looked to him as the taste maker, always in the right place at the right time."

When President Kennedy had a birthday celebration at Madison Square Garden in 1963, Blackwell, who was part of the organizing team, called Brody asking him to participate. Brody agreed to have the Four Seasons host a pre-birthday dinner for 450 of the major Democratic donors. On the day of the celebration, Dorothy Kilgallen, the right-wing syndicated political columnist, criticized the administration for using government funds to pay for a trip to Washington made by Stuart Levin, then a manager of the Four Seasons, to discuss the menu for the pre-birthday dinner. No such trip had been made, no money had exchanged hands, and the Four Seasons consulted with no one to select the dinner.

As Brody waited for the President at the 52nd Street entrance to the Four Seasons, he remembered having addressed his staff just after the restaurant had opened, saying half in jest that "This restaurant will achieve its appropriate status only when the President of the United States comes to dinner." Now at 5:30 PM on a very hot spring day, Brody, standing at curbside on East 52nd Street, awaited the arrival of President Kennedy.

Kennedy was driven up to the curb in an open convertible. He was alone in the convertible and without a police escort. Brody and the President shook hands, and then the President said, "What did you think of the Kilgallen article?" Brody, startled and amused by the President's acuity, replied, "Who reads Kilgallen?"

As Brody led the President up the stairs into the restaurant, a man was descending the stairs; he and the President smiled at one another. The President said, "This has been a great day for you." He recognized the man as Kenny Steinbach who was the head of the Ruppert Brewery. On a sweltering day like that one, New Yorkers must have gone through a lot of Kenny Steinbach's beer.

Once inside the restaurant, Brody asked the President if he wanted to visit the kitchen—this despite the fact that the Secret Service had declared the kitchen off limits. Yes, the President wanted to visit the kitchen. He said, "That's where all the Democrats are."

When the President entered, the kitchen staff had formed a reception line and the President shook everyone's hand. Stopping in front of an Asian, the President asked how he liked America. Brody figured that the kitchen staff who were eligible to vote had just made their election day decision final.

Kennedy was not scheduled to eat, but that did not stop Brody. He asked if the President would dine and the President gladly accepted. Brody showed the President to a private dining room up a level from the Grill Room and Bar and seated him alone at a large table.

Brody said he would arrange for some wait staff. He then collared Pierre Salinger and asked what the President would eat. When Brody returned to the private dining room, Kennedy's table was filled with members of the in crowd, such as Arthur Krim and Anne Rosenberg.

When it was time for Kennedy to leave for Madison Square Garden, he passed by the table where Brody was dining with his wife, his sister, and his brother-in-law. He smiled at Brody and said, "So this is the family table." He then invited the Brody party to Madison Square Garden.

Among the 450 Democratic donors, there were many VIPs who until the pre-birthday dinner had not known of the Four Seasons. From that moment on, many of them made it their favorite restaurant—and they told their friends who told their friends, etc.

The Four Seasons began getting more requests for reservations than it had space. And, along with the crowds, success bred some embarrassments. Arthur "Punch" Sulzberger, owner of he *New York Times* showed up for lunch without a reservation, and the *maitre d'* kicked him out. (The Forum of the Twelve Caesars, also at the red hot center of things, not to be outdone in the *gaffe* category, failed to seat John D. Rockefeller 3rd because "the place was too crowded." (Brody remembers "taking it a lot worse than John D.")

RA was growing in size and complexity and Brody divided it into separate divisions, each with its own supervisor. Brody was chief executive officer and Joe Baum executive vice-president, who had responsibility for running the Four Seasons. Mimi Sheraton, who was later to conduct menu and recipe research for the Four Seasons, described Baum as "the madly creative restaurateur" and Brody as "the intensely practical financial man." Baum would inspire many distinguished chefs, but his compulsive perfectionism sometimes diverted his attention from the financial underpinnings of the business. The steely focus of a man like Brody was a necessary complement to Baum's mercurial talent.

When Brody was forced out of the Restaurant Associates empire in September 1963, Joe Baum was the most illustrious survivor of the Brody era and garnered to himself much of the praise for the pre-eminence of the great days of Restaurant Associates. An article in GQ heaped such lavish and unearned praise on Baum, that Brody's former wife Grace whom he had not heard from in many years called him to share with him her distress that Baum had been allowed to pirate Brody's achievements. When Baum died in 1998, his obituary in the *New York Times* praised him for his showman's genius and his profound understanding of food and how to market it to RA's customers. He deserved all that praise. He was also praised for being the force behind the creation of the real estate, the architecture and aesthetics, and the financial success of RA. But those achievements belong to Brody and the team he assembled of which Baum was just a part. Brody was written out of the RA saga and Baum was written in. It was a triumph of Baum's showmanship over Brody's substance. By the time the restaurant publicity engine bestowed the virtue of RA's greatness on Joe Baum, Brody was no longer there to influence the flow of propaganda. He was doing other things by then.

The Brasserie,
Mama Leone's,
La Fonda del Sol

Fifty-third Street between Park and Lexington Avenues forms the north boundary of the Seagram Building. Until the opening of the Brasserie, no other retail shop existed in that block, and, therefore, when Seagram made the space available, Brody wondered how any restaurant would succeed with no passersby. Nonetheless, Brody's mandate was to build a second restaurant adjoining the Four Seasons. Executives from the Rikers team traveled to France to examine the feasibility of a French "brasserie" in New York. The Brasserie would be next door to the Four Seasons and it was likely that it would inherit some of its clout.

Brody opened the Brasserie as a 24-hour luxury coffee shop, which served gourmet breakfasts, wine and spirits, quick snacks or fine food, put it under the operational control of the Rikers group and serviced it out of the Rikers commissary. With the help of American Express Card promotional money, the Brasserie became a great success, introducing Americans to a particularly enjoyable but largely unfamiliar style of French casual snacking and dining.

One Sunday evening, Brody and his management team were meeting at the Forum, when Gene Leone, the owner of the New

York landmark restaurant Mama Leone's, walked in for dinner and joined them for a chat. A few days later, Leone called Brody to tell him that Mama Leone's was for sale. Even before learning the actual operating numbers, Brody knew that the restaurant was a gold mine. In fact it was doing $3 million annual sales and $750,000 pre-tax operating profits.

Leone had become fed up with his two sons-in-law, who he did not think worked hard enough. Against financial and familial commonsense, Leone had decided to sell. Brody knew that despite all of RA's creativity and inventiveness, it had never seen numbers like those achieved by Mama Leone's and considered the opportunity to buy Mama Leone's an incredible bit of good fortune.

Brody began negotiations wondering where he would get the necessary financing without having to surrender equity. Since the deal would include the real estate on which Mama Leone's stood, a cousin of Brody's suggested he talk with Larry Wien, an important player in New York commercial real estate.

With Wien as an ally, Brody had modified his proposal so that an all-cash deal of $2.5 million was on the table. Not having such a bankroll, Brody suggested to Wien that Wien buy the property and then lease it back to Brody, who would pay $235,000 per year for a 10-year lease with ten 10-year options. Cost of Living Increases (CLI's) had not become a business custom in the early 1960s and no increases were negotiated into the contract; it was one rent forever. Wien would put up $1.5 million in cash. Brody would have to get the other million from a bank.

Wien was happy to make such a deal. There was enough in it for him to get a management fee, and he could easily finance the upfront money. Brody, on the other hand, had trouble with his bank, which would not lend him the million unless Brody found somebody to do what the banker called a "Takeout Agreement."

This person would not sign the note, but would promise *to take the bank out* of the million dollars within a year. Brody went to Wien with the proposition and Wien agreed. He knew that Mama Leone's was making $750,000 a year and that Brody's other operations were in the black.

Because Mama Leone's was such a successful operation, Brody and his team were not about to make any major changes. Gene Leone had agreed to stay on for six months after the sale in order to smooth the transition, but the day finally came for Brody and his team to take over. They collected the whole crew upstairs, and Gene Leone started the meeting by wishing everybody good luck and bidding them goodbye. Brody then welcomed them to their new family. Brody remembers that he felt instant warmth from them. It was only later that he found out that the warmth was probably from relief, because Leone had made himself widely disliked.

Christmas was coming and Brody decided to put up lavishly decorative lighting on the exterior of the building. Very late one afternoon, as Brody was leaving the restaurant, he walked to the parking lot and the attendant brought Brody's car to him and said, "Hey, you know Leone was here the other day. And I said to him. 'You see all those lights on the building—all that Christmas stuff. It took a Jew to do that.'"

Mama Leone's performed just as expected. Brody was able to cover the cost of the financing by opening on Sundays. The acquisition of Mama Leone's had a monumental impact on RA. Not only were there tremendous profits, but it provided the cash flow needed for the marketing of the Four Seasons and the almost simultaneous planning and execution of La Fonda del Sol.

At a time when the fate of the Four Seasons was still being decided, Brody committed his RA team to the development of another great restaurant, which even aficionados of the Four

Seasons recognized as its equal in ambition and some thought, its superior in beauty. As he had in seeking out Brody to rent space in Rockefeller Center for the Forum of the Twelve Caesars, Gus Eyssell, in charge of Rockefeller Center real estate development, encouraged Brody to develop a great restaurant in the Time-Life Building.

Brody employed the design services of Alexander H. Girard, who spent seven weeks in Central and South America searching for themes and *objets d'art*. La Fonda del Sol contained a bar which was actually an adobe hut (with forty or so window niches) set up inside, each filled with filigreed metal toys from Mexico, figures of Diablada dancers from Brazil, a Colombian parakeet, Guatemalan dolls, birdcages, toy musical instruments, and market place objects. There was an entire wall of food and drink signs in Spanish and Portuguese.

To justify its name (Inn of the Sun) Girard made lavish use of highly original sun symbols, all created exclusively for La Fonda del Sol and ranging from an 11-foot brass mural in the bar lounge to tiny emblems on the match books and cocktail napkins. Splashes of wild radiant color, with flame tones seeming to predominate, further carried out the celebratory sun motif. The interior construction used woods from Brazil and floor tiles and marbles from Cuba. The centerpiece of La Fonda was an enormous rotisserie attended by chefs in white hats. As one critic remarked, "None of RA's success would be possible, of course, without a terrifyingly rigid adherence to the most basic principle of all in the restaurant business: superb food served in a manner to which everyone would like to become accustomed."

The Four Seasons and La Fonda were the beginning of a metamorphosis of the whole company made possible in large part by the liquidity afforded by Mama Leone's. For Brody, growth was an essential part of his vision. Multiple deluxe restaurants, not only in America, but also in Europe were part of his vision of RA's future. In order for that to happen it would be necessary to leverage RA's dramatic growth by folding the cash flow and bottom line revenues of Mama Leone's into the balance sheet of the rest of RA. Then the operation might be sound enough to qualify for an IPO (initial public offering), and that is what Brody's father's attorney Albert Parker of Parker, Chapin & Flattau suggested.

Brody was skeptical that anyone would underwrite the IPO, but Albert Parker brought Brody to the offices of Shearson Hammil and introduced him to Stan Kruzen its senior officer. It was Brody's first exposure to the machinations of public offerings, and he enjoyed his education. And, as Brody remembers, so did Shearson Hammil, who in their protracted due process efforts enjoyed endless meals at the Four Seasons.

When news of Brody's plans to seek an IPO became known in the restaurant community, the great Henri Soulé approached Brody, suggesting that his restaurants become part of the Brody offering. Brody was highly complimented by Soulé's interest. Soulé had established the benchmark for great French dining in America with the opening of Le Pavillion at the 1939 New York World's Fair. When the War in Europe left Soulé stranded in America, he established himself as the country's finest restaurateur. At the time of the RA planned IPO, Soulé's fame, however, was far more solid than the financial basis of his restaurant organization.

Soulé invited Brody to lunch at his exquisitely beautiful La Côte Basque, where lunch included large heaps of caviar and pink champagne, and the agenda was the inclusion of the Soulé properties in the Restaurant Associates IPO. But the financial numbers showed that only La Côte Basque was doing well, and that Soulé's grand restaurant in East Hampton, The Hedges, was a disaster. With much regret Brody could not invite an alliance with Soulé, especially at a time when RA itself was not without weaknesses.

To the underwriter, the down side of RA was that it owned very little and showed only small profits. However, it had strong growth and was glamorous. In 1961, it seemed that the bullish public would buy up almost any decent offering. Shearson set a date for the public offering.

In the meanwhile, Brody had gotten the notion that European airports offered an opportunity for the same kind of hotel and restaurant development that had been successful in the United States. Over drinks at the Four Seasons with Fred Waechter, a relative of his in-laws who lived in Geneva, Brody described his interest in developing such business. Before the IPO, Brody got a call from Fred who told him to come to Geneva at once, because the Geneva airport itself was about to concession a hotel. Brody traveled immediately to Geneva, but discovered that the concession had already been granted.

While that news was disappointing, Brody discovered that Waechter had important contacts among French real estate developers and builders. In the course of the Geneva negotiations, Brody let on that he would be interested in Paris. That hint fell on fertile ground, but before it yielded fruit, Brody returned to New York for the IPO.

Shearson Hammil brought RA out at $11 and did a $3 million offering. Restaurant Associates became Restaurant Associates Industries. On the death of Philip Wechsler several years earlier, Brody, himself, owned 10% of the stock, and his wife and three children, a combined 42%. Together they sold a small amount of their stock and put it into a small investment partnership. Although he was not happily married, Brody had never contemplated divorce. He accepted the division of stock as it was offered, never dreaming that one day he would lose it all.

Brody continued to push for expansion. He negotiated with Louis Wolfson, who owned the Pan Am building, for Charley Brown's. Then, in order to reflect the Italian and German destinations of Pan Am's flights, Brody patterned Trattoria and Zum Zum on authentic European models.

Brody was not going to let RA become stereotyped. While he did not think he could compete at the level of French cuisine represented by a Henri Soulé, he could offer cafeterias, coffee shops, and various theme restaurants that made up an ensemble of dining possibilities in huge complexes like the Pan Am Building or the Time-Life buildings.

Brody had found a void, an opportunity, in the urgent needs of major post-War commercial landlords. The success of RA's dining ensembles re-invented the New York restaurant business, moving it from individually-owned stores, which depended on the labor of family owners and faithful retainers, to a professionally trained and financed group of business entrepreneurs in touch with the latest culinary developments and eager for growth and innovation.

Even in the glow, perhaps, even in the *heat* of RA's dramatic public acclaim, Brody knew that RA's growth and its future were more a matter of individual opportunities than a formulaic master plan. He told Gilbert Millstein of *Esquire*,

> There is a certain restless drive in me that all of us have. I don't have the ambition to become the prime restaurateur in the world *per se*, but I *do* have the normal capitalist tendency to make money and build up a strong company....We do it mostly by opportunity and the experience gained from what we've done previously. Once you get started, the very elements that started you out push you. Right now, I don't know where

we're going. I don't feel any big emotional need for another place. And, you know, I still have no great feeling that we have the touch.

For Brody, the only way to find out was to continue doing.

Brody missed one growth possibility. It was in hindsight, in his own estimation, the biggest opportunity—the franchising of Rikers. But the concept of franchising lay in the future. In any case, even without franchising, Brody would find much to do to broaden RA's base of operations and that was to be in Europe.

Brody's interest in doing business in Europe was in part triggered by the relationship he established with Time-Life while creating the Tower Suite and La Fonda del Sol in the Time-Life Building. When Time-Life decided to put a restaurant in its Paris office building on the Rue Rabelais, they asked RA to develop the design and run the operation. The design work was put into the hands of Raymond Loewy, who developed the plans for a steak house with an American Old West theme. When Brody established offices in Paris as part of the Divonne venture, his team was in place to manage the Time-Life Paris steak house. But by that time, the Divonne negotiations had taken over as the most important step towards European expansion.

The Team

Running concurrently with the eye-catching center pieces of the RA empire, the Forum and the Four Seasons, or about to be added to them, were other substantial RA operations. There were the Rikers coffee shops and cafeterias, commissaries at Mitchell and Griffis Air Force bases, the New York State Thruway business, Newark Airport operations, the John Peel English Pub and Restaurant in Westbury, Long Island, the commissary and restaurant business for Orbach's Department Store in New York City, the Brasserie, the Pan Am Building operations, including the Trattoria, Charley Brown's, and Zum Zum, the Time-Life Building operations, including La Fonda del Sol and Tower Suite, and Mama Leone's.

Brody needed to build a superb home-office team, which he put under the direction of Austin Cox. Not only was Cox in on the hiring process, but he did on-site evaluations. He was mandated to build up files for the future recruiting, which would be necessary in RA's ambitious growth stage.

In the creation of Brody's most dramatic and superb restaurants, the Forum, the Four Seasons, La Fonda, Brody's executive team gained a reputation for being almost frighteningly intelligent. The great interior designer William Pahlmann, whose first commission from Brody was the Forum of the Twelve Caesars, called them "...smart cookies. Charm boys. They are so analytical. They explore a thing right down to the ground." They also were in harmony with Brody's grand designs and his feel for where New York society was heading. Gilbert Millstein in *Esquire* said that they were ,

> . . . firmly founded in a secure corner of that peculiar, uneven terrain over which Culture and *Kitsch* ordinarily stage murderous forced marches against each other. The fact is that the organization's executives are quite expert, if humorous, social observers and acutely aware that they are living in a period of transition so violent that the new rich, the old rich, the aspiring rich on expense accounts, the hounds of sensibility, the new *cognoscenti* of food, wine and décor, the merely curious affluent and the desperate scramblers for social preference of one kind or another have all been ushered willy-nilly into the same anteroom, so to speak, to wait anxiously for a choice table.

This team had been built slowly and at first had less grand items on its agenda than the creation of RA's trend-setting grand dining establishments. When Brody first joined the company, RA had a commissary on West 27th Street in a building they owned, in which RA baked, cooked, and distributed food to Rikers and the other cafeterias. A profitable real estate opportunity arose to sell the old building and to buy another one very cheaply. It was a large building on West 57th Street between 10th and 11th Avenues, which became RA's office and new commissary.

When Brody was in town. all information came back to him directly on a daily basis, and, usually, face-to-face. But as RA spread out from installation to installation, there were more places in need of supervision. Each restaurant had a manager with responsibility for recruiting, research, and original menus and their modification and improvement. In all of these activities, Brody also was actively involved.

Brody was particularly vigilant in not allowing his personal taste or the personal tastes of his executives and managers to intervene in the success of a restaurant. More than what the restaurateur himself liked, it was what was popular on the menu that molded the cuisine of RA's restaurants. Mechanisms for acquiring that information on a daily basis were set up, and every restaurant manager was expected to be alert to any changes.

Though Brody welcomed the opinions of his executives and his chefs about the foods served at the restaurant, Brody never ceded his final authority in matters of the taste buds even to Joe Baum. Some people are blessed with extra powerful eyesight, others with the perfect nose, others with superior hearing. Brody has unerringly true taste buds. It is a gift he discovered, at of all places, the Rikers cafeterias.

Rikers offered no menus. Each customer might come into the shop and order only one thing. Whether it was a cup of coffee or an apple, it had to be good enough that the customer's memory of the visit turned into such a rewarding taste sensation that he wanted to return to Rikers. Each individual item, humble though it might be, needed to be perfect. Food selection, even at the best of the RA restaurants, with Joe Baum in charge, was open to discussion, but was never a New England town meeting.

Key personnel included George Arnold, an engineer, who RA recruited away from the restaurant equipment manufacturer, Strauss Duparquet. Arnold was an expert in equipping and laying out commercial kitchens, and, at RA, he eventually assumed a post as head of all engineering and construction .

Joe Lapin was a holdover from the old RA in the early days of Rikers and the cafeterias, and was the financial controller, who reported directly to Brody and to Brody only.

Lee Jaffe had been with RA since the 1940s, and was the purchasing agent for non-food items.

Philip Miles worked his public relations magic.

Lester Klepper had been house counsel to Orbach's. When Orbach's moved uptown to 42nd Street, Brody learned that they were searching for someone to run a lunchroom in their store; Brody recognized that this opportunity fit into the RA formula for landlord friendliness and could be modeled on RA's Rikers operations. Seeking to land the Orbach's cafeteria franchise, Brody, in negotiating the deal, found himself opposite Lester Klepper, and was taken with his friendliness, conscientiousness and intelligence. He induced Klepper to join RA, where he would have the legal responsibilities for lease negotiations, labor negotiations, and, more than any other person, work with Brody on potential new ventures.

Mike Warfel, whom Brody had met when Warfel ran a department of the hotel and restaurant auditors, Harris, Kerr, Forster, when they were consulting for the New York State Thruway Authority, was brought in to help RA expand into the restaurant management business, the particular domain of the Management Group.

Brody became re-acquainted with Warfel, when Harry Helmsley asked RA to manage the John Peel Restaurant in Westbury, Long Island on a management fee basis plus incentives. Brody asked Warfel to come to RA. When they visited the offices of the John Peel's designer, Warfel looked at the work, and the first thing he said to the staff was "Everything has to be changed. We have to start over." Brody was impressed.

But more than individual management contracts, Brody was

looking for chain-wide deals such as those achieved by some of the major hotel companies, who were awarded lucrative contracts without having to put up any cash equity. Warfel's hiring signaled RA's desire to share in this kind of arrangement. Warfel's accounting background and his familiarity with such operations around the world were key to the plans of Management Group, but its ambitious plans were not to be fulfilled.

Brody and Warfel made a deal to design, construct, and manage the Tower Suite at the top of the Time-Life Building. For that particular project Brody had hired George Nelson. But just after the project began, Warfel decided to leave RA for a better opportunity as food and beverage director of the Sheraton Hotel Group. Management Group was left with the operation of Tower Suite and the John Peel, but without a manager with sufficient time and expertise for those tasks or the much larger one of bringing the strategic objectives of Management Group to fruition.

Brody's mind was already set on European expansion. Joe Baum, who was a compulsive workacholic, and already had too much to do, took over Warfel's responsibilities. It proved to be too much of a load. Baum suffered a nervous breakdown.

Divonne-les-Bains

The French real estate developers whom Brody had met in Geneva called him from Paris early in 1961. They told Brody that Orly airport was being considered for development. Brody left for Paris at once and spent three days and nights at their Paris offices developing a presentation and a rough plan for the hotel that they would develop at Orly.

Brody and the French developers attended a meeting of the Paris Airport board. The senior partner of the French company, SEFRI, Jean Claude Aaron, made a memorable presentation, spiced with humor, showing his comfort with the French old-boy network. Their plan was to have SEFRI build the airport hotel and RA operate it.

On one of the nights that they were working on their presentation, Brody saw an old map spread out on an unused desk. He said, "With all the great new highways that are under construction and which are in planning in Europe, there ought to be a serious opportunity along those routes and entrances for restaurants." Brody's remarks were carefully noted.

Neither the French development company nor RA were to get the Orly business. Brody was notified in March that the board had selected Hilton. In June, Brody received a call from Jean François Rozan, one of the partners in the French development company, telling him that they had found an opportunity along a new highway that was being built from Geneva to Lausanne, with an off ramp at Divonne-les-Bains.

The property at Divonne-les-Bains included two hotels and a casino. For the deal, the French developer would act as RA's agent, and, if Brody were successful, receive a finder's fee.

Brody traveled to France and visited Divonne, where he met with Fleury Creton, the resident partner of the hotel and casino operation, who provided Brody with the financials expressed in French francs. The combined operations seemed to gross $3 million and generate $700,000 yearly cash flow. Brody promptly took them to the Paris branch of Price Waterhouse in order to put the financials into a form with which American financial institutions would be familiar.

The operation consisted of two small hotels, a golf course, a thermal bath, a theater, and a casino. which was not only making a profit of $600,000 per year, but had $700,000 in cash and had no debt or mortgage. The asking price was $3 million. To Brody it was an attractive purchase, which could be financed through debt.

Brody went to the Paris offices of Lazard Fréres, who liked the numbers and thought the business was a good one, but who did not want to participate because the puritanical Lazard Fréres did not want to associate their name with a gambling operation.

In subsequent months, Brody embarked on a round of visits to various banks in Geneva and Paris in pursuit of debt financing. When in Paris, Brody used the offices of his real estate developer friends, SEFRI, from the Orly Airport attempt. On one of those occasions, Brody brought to Paris with him Walter Maynard, a partner from Shearson Hammil and Albert Parker,

Brody's attorney. Brody took them to Divonne to examine the property and to discuss the whole project.

Maynard suggested financing the deal by issuing more RA stock, but Brody was against the resulting dilution, much preferring debt financing. Shearson Hammil was not open to the debt strategy.

Brody approached some real estate people in New York, including Larry Wien, who had made the Leone's deal possible. Simultaneous with Brody's approach to Wien, France was plunged into the middle of the OAS Algerian crisis, and foreign investors were wary of French investments. Brody was forced to wait; the problem was how to keep the sellers confident that RA was going to proceed. The sellers suggested a way, asking Brody to come up with $300,000 in "sincere" money.

Brody got an introduction to the Morgan Guaranty Bank, where Abraham Claude, Jr. arranged the $300,000 loan for Brody against his own Restaurant Associates stock. Morgan Guaranty would not loan the money to the company, preferring Brody's personal worth to reliance on a Wechsler-controlled corporation.

The Paris law firm of Cleary Gottlieb drafted an agreement for Brody so that under any conditions, if RA did not close the Divonne deal by a certain date, Brody could get his money back. Towards the end of April, Jean Claude Aaron called Brody in New York to say that his firm had arranged the financing for the entire $3 million. But under those circumstances, his firm wanted 50% equity. Brody agreed.

Aaron's firm had raised the $3 million by getting three different insurance companies to invest $1 million each. The insurance companies then took their $1 million"put" each to a different bank and borrowed a million each against each "put." It impressed Brody as being "as complicated as if they were buying Manhattan." The banks would have neither equity in property nor any share in the development. If the venture failed, the insurance companies would own the property.

In order to impress the French insurance companies and banks that RA and Aaron's firm were jointly making this loan, Brody and Aaron had presented a company that planned to expand all around Europe, and, in order to make that seem plausible, the firm needed a Paris office and a new name: "Compagnie Française des Grands Hotels Internationaux (CFGHI)." Aaron had a candidate to be its president.

Germain Vidal was Prefect of the Seine et Marne Départment. He was part of the French "old boy" network, without whom it is almost impossible to do business in France. The prefecture was in fact a small palace in Fontainebleau, appointed and operated in regal style.

Aaron and Brody dined excellently at the prefecture, with Aaron doing the translating. After dinner, Brody and Vidal retired to a private room, where the two men discussed—in their limited understanding of one another's language—the terms of Vidal's employment, including how much salary he would receive.

The next morning, Aaron called Brody and told him how upset he was with how Brody had treated Vidal. Brody did not understand, until Aaron said that Brody had not offered to pay Vidal enough money. Brody, recognizing that he was now caught up in a murky game of his new partners' devising, adjusted Vidal's salary upward. That was the beginning of the education he would get in the *modus operandi* of the French old boy network, a difference of attitude towards business procedures that was much deeper than a difference in language.

They hired Vidal. He was eager to join the new firm since the French government had told him that if he did not give up his prefecture he could be reassigned to war torn Algeria.

Casinos were virtually branches of the French government. Every detail was under government control. There had never before been a non-French organization allowed ownership in a French casino. The influence that a man like Vidal was able to wield behind the scenes would be crucial to Brody's plans.

As the closing date approached, Brody was notified that the new company needed someone to run the Paris office, a multi-lingual, super-efficient office manager. They had a candidate for the job. She turned out to be Marlene Gray, the future Mrs. Brody.

Before Brody made the acquaintance of the new Paris office manager, his partners suggested that CFGHI rent office space in a building his partners already owned. When Brody refused, Jean Claude Aaron said, "But the bank wants you to rent this space." Brody asked, "What bank?" The bank Aaron named was one of the three banks from which Aaron and his partners had borrowed the money to finance the Divonne-les-Bains purchase. Brody wanted to meet with this banker and Aaron had no objection.

At the meeting, the banker asked Brody if he had any questions about the choice of location for the new CFGHI office. He looked at Brody and wondered aloud if there was some problem. Brody said there was not, but sensing that Aaron was using CFGHI to covertly repay the bankers who had been friendly to their enterprise, Brody said that he would like to see the loan agreement. Amazingly enough he was told that there was no loan agreement. Brody recognized that it had been a deal done informally among Jean Claude Aaron's "old boys," the insurance companies' "old boys," and the bankers' "old boys." By the time Brody left the bank's offices, the bank had given up its insistence on having the offices of CFGHI in a building owned by Aaron's company. Brody knew that if he had walked into that bank with the same deal and wanted to borrow 10 cents, they would not have done business with him. In France, things did not work that way.

As he had done previously with staff members when they were given assignments in areas with which they were unfamiliar, Brody thought it crucial that Vidal and Marlene Gray acquaint themselves with casino operations in Las Vegas and Puerto Rico before becoming involved in the operations at Divonne.

Mr. and Mrs. Vidal and Marlene Gray headed for America and their training in the casino-hotel business. Brody and Marlene met for the first time at Idlewild (now JFK) airport in New York. Vidal and Marlene were given a tour of the RA New York operations. Alan Lewis of the RA executive group volunteered to be the resident manager of Divonne. Brody approved, assigning Lewis to accompany the Vidals and Gray to Puerto Rico, Miami, Los Angeles, and Las Vegas, and, when the tour was over, to send them back to Paris.

Shortly thereafter, CFGHI took title to the Divonne-les-Bains properties. Germain Vidal was to be the master of ceremonies for the change in ownership and was to introduce Brody and his partners to the crew of the casino. But Vidal had been delayed and did not show up. Alan Lewis enraged. "What are we going to do?" he shouted at Brody." Brody told Lewis to take it easy. Brody would do it himself. So they assembled the crew, and Brody in his pigeon French welcomed everyone.

Later that afternoon, Aaron and Brody went to Geneva and the Banque de l'Harpe and got title to the Divonne properties, and turned over $3 million to the sellers. It was May 28, 1962. For about eighteen months Wall Street had been in a bear market. On that day, skittish investors saw the Dow Jones average close at 611; it had lost more than 3% of its value, a percentage drop which if applied to a year 2000 Dow Jones valued at more than 10,000, would amount to more than a 300-point loss. For the first night of the new ownership, the casino was empty. The setback of Monday proved temporary and regular business revived almost immediately. For the next year, the casino operated as predicted; although, Alan Lewis's introduction to his Divonne management duties was stressful. When the mayor of the village, who also held the French cabinet post of Commissioner of Gaming and Tourism, suggested that Lewis hire the mayor's girlfriend to sing in the Divonne nightclub, Lewis auditioned her and declined her talents. Soon the gendarmes arrived to place Lewis in handcuffs; Brody was forced to arrange for Lewis's release. Not surprisingly, the mayor's girlfriend got to sing in the nightclub.

Otherwise, the casino operation ran smoothly. RA kept the gambling concession with the group that had been running it previously. There was nothing much to do except bank the profits, particularly from the oligarch's game in which the casino specialized, a no-limits version of *chemin de fer* called "*banque a tout va*" favored by Arab oil sheiks.

Divorce

The many trips to Europe that were part of the acquisition of Divonne strengthened Brody's vision of a Restaurant Associates expanded by a strong European operation. Brody tried to interest Grace in bringing the children to Paris for six months, but she would not do it. Club social activities were at the center of her life. In the midst of the acquisition of Divonne-les-Bains, Grace called Brody in Europe, not to inquire about the progress of the deal, but to remind him to be back in Scarsdale by Friday so that he would not miss a club party. This time the schism between the Brodys had become deep.

During the several trips Brody made to Europe on Divonne and Time-Life business, he had explored venues for future restaurant and hotel sites. A trip to Italy uncovered an abandoned medieval convent, which he had visions of converting into an historic destination restaurant. Brody's main interest in RA had evolved into the creation, rather than the acquisition, of new businesses. This creative agenda promised to give full expression to his conceptual genius.

Just as the acquisition of Mama Leone's had provided the cashflow necessary to set such glamorous operations as the Four

Seasons and La Fonda del Sol into motion, Divonne-les-Bains could provide the financial *bona fides* for European expansion— just the kind of debt financing that would preserve RA's equity position.

It was fortunate for Brody that once Divonne had been acquired, it did not require much of his attention. The casino, after all, was run as a concession and the trusted Alan Lewis was on-site as the full-time manager. Brody's attention was needed to quarterback the New York operations.

At the time of the Divonne acquisition, in May 1962, RA was doing $35 million annually, a substantial sum for that period. Even without Divonne, in January 1961, RA's financial statement—strong in growth, not so strong in profit—was sufficient for Shearson to succeed in the initial public offering of Restaurant Associates stock and to get the company listed on the American Stock Exchange

In 1961, Restaurant Associates became a successful public offering. That weekend, Brody and Grace attended another dance at the club. Of course, Brody was glad-handed and congratulated by his fellow capitalists. With the joy and fulfillment that should have been his painfully missing, Brody looked out over the crowd of Quaker Ridge club mates and thought to himself, "Ah! so this is what it's like being rich." It was no fun at all.

Simultaneous with the Divonne negotiations and acquisition, RA was completing the construction of La Fonda del Sol in Rockefeller Center; it also achieved a management and fee contract for the Tower Suite. Time-Life also chose RA to design and manage—again on a fee basis—a restaurant it would build and own in its Paris headquarters on the Rue Rabelais. Time-Life would pay all construction costs and give Brody his choice of designers. Brody chose designer Raymond Loewy, and work began on the steak restaurant Le Western, so-named to appeal to the French infatuation with American Western movies.

The same combination of financial backing and aesthetic independence that had resulted in the triumph of the Four Seasons made prospects for Le Western bright indeed. When Brody was forced out of RA, the concept and many of the design details were acquired by Hilton and used in their Paris Hilton.

As an additional bonus, Brody, who already had a Paris-based office as a result of his partnership with CFGHI in the Divonne deal, would need to be in Paris often to oversee the Time-Life project, enabling him to explore other European venues.

The Four Seasons was going full tilt, generating as much press and culinary comment as any other restaurant in America. RA-owned Mama Leone's had never done better business. The Brasserie had opened to rave reviews and, snuggled alongside the Four Seasons at the Seagram Building, created the impression that RA was the hottest restaurant operator in New York.

The enormous talent pool needed to run these new operations rested with Austin Cox, who, as mentioned, was one of Brody's first hires. Cox set up his department and was recruiting constantly.

Also at this time, Brody approached Louis Wolfson and his associates at the Pan Am building about creating several levels of restaurants for the cavernous Pan Am building. Brody had three restaurants in mind; one of them would be a showpiece restaurant on the top floor of the Pan Am Building. In his mind's eye, Brody thought of it as the "Pearl of the Orient." Driving down Park Avenue, he pictured the great monolith of the Pan Am Building wearing near its head a figurative jewel in its imperial turban. But this time Brody's reach exceeded RA's grasp. Wolfson and his associates, unlike the landlords in the earlier ventures of RA, were not so generous with the now glittery RA.

If RA wanted to open a new restaurant, it would have to use its own money. It had become hard for Brody to plead poverty.

When, finally, RA discovered that it did not have the ability to finance all three restaurants, Brody had to ask Wolfson for a re-hearing. He expected to lose two restaurants. But Wolfson and his associates agreed to have RA proceed with Trattoria and Zum Zum, both of which were soon up, running, and successful.

But if RA could no longer plead poverty, it could definitely plead anxiety. The cafeterias had grown old and expensive. Built when New York City rents were low, each lease renewal escalated until the stores were too expensive. In addition to rising rents, the cafeterias had been unionized. Eventually RA closed the central preparation commissary, eliminating along with that operation the necessity of paying for union trucking. RA tried to operate the restaurants on their own, but while a few Rikers, such as the one on 6th Avenue and 57th street were beautifully renovated, the cafeteria business was moribund. In fact, for the city as a whole, the era of the cafeteria had come to an end.

The management operation, begun with Mike Warfel, with his defection, stagnated. There was little executive time or enthusiasm left to develop the management side of the business. The restaurants along the New York State Thruway, the Tower Suite in the Time-Life Building and the Long Island John Peele of Harry Helmsley and Larry Wien were the last management operations run by RA under Brody.

Even the prestige restaurants, as crowded as they were and as much in the news, went through cycles of financial success accompanied by cash flow problems. The launch of a restaurant like the Four Seasons is inevitably saddled with initial negative cash flow. It takes time until staff knows what it is doing. During the shakedown period, more help is hired than will eventually be needed. Food is wasted. Control is often missing. The expensive publicity and promotion campaign to get recognition and guests is at its most fervid and expensive.

When Brody bought Leone's, RA acquired a going business. The operational plan was not to ruin it, but to leave it alone as much as possible. However, as rewarding as acquiring a cashflow fountain as Mama Leone's was, the real excitement and reward for Brody was in creating restaurants. It was also a lot more dangerous.

As large as RA was becoming, it was difficult, if not impossible, to calculate how big the operating budget had become. The big concern was how much was left. Cashflow was king, not the size of the equity investment. RA had reached a point that in order to improve its cashflow, a new project was always required. Brody and his executives felt that the next project would always pull them out. They thought the savior this time was Divonne-les-Bains.

But there was a bigger threat to Brody's empire from which even Divonne was no protection. At long last, Grace and Brody candidly discussed divorce. The Wechsler family, which included Grace's sister Elaine and Jimmy Slater, Grace's brother-in-law, were part of the circle discussing the divorce and promoting it. During the first year of the Divonne operation, they went as far as recommending a divorce lawyer to Grace. The question was no longer if the Brodys would divorce, but when.

The Wechsler clan agreed that they would sell out to Brody. It appeared that they wanted to have nothing more to do with a business in which they had never taken interest nor tried to understand. Brody could imagine RA in no one else's hands but his own.

Ever since he first took over the Rikers operation, Brody had considered himself RA's boss and the Wechsler's had done little to make him think he was wrong. For Brody, Restaurant Associates was his. "It was all me. There was no other association."

Brody had set himself up for a cruel surprise. In the end, when the family had decided not to do business with him, they would use his pride against him. So identified was he with his captaincy of Restaurant Associates, he failed to acknowledge that he had always been treated as a foreigner among the tight-knit Wechsler clan into whose hands the control of RA's destiny could revert anytime they chose.

Brody, believing correctly that they could not make the empire work without him, but not seeing that other considerations were more relevant to the Wechslers than Brody's vision of RA, walked self-destructively into the ambush that inevitably awaited him as a result of his and Grace's incompatibility.

Once the whole Wechsler family accepted the idea of a divorce as inevitable, Grace and Jerry negotiated a separation agreement. Brody brought in his long time friend, Carl Hess, to advise him on the negotiations and to raise the money. Hess's financial genius was considerable. As an executive of American Securities, a successful private investment firm, founded and controlled by the Rosenwald family, Hess arranged for American Securities to make Brody a $2.5 million loan, which would be guaranteed by Rockefeller Center. Carl Hess shortly afterwards founded AEA which became the largest investment partnership in the world. Shearson Hammil negotiated on Brody's behalf with Abe Wechsler and the deal was agreed upon.

At almost the same moment that Grace and Brody signed their separation agreement, the Wechslers cut off further talks and told Brody to get out. They would not sell to him.

It is tempting to think that this change of mind was caused by the animus the Wechslers had towards the man who had made Grace unhappy. But a more compelling reason existed. Jimmy Slater and Martin Brody, without the knowledge of Brody, had acquired Waldorf Systems for between $35 and 40 million and had persuaded the Wechslers to merge Waldorf with Restaurant Associates. That such a massive acquisition and crucial strategic step for Restaurant Associates could be negotiated without Brody's knowledge was flaming proof that the Wechslers had a far different notion of Brody's place in the RA empire than did Brody.

For many reasons, the Waldorf merger was unattractive—even perverse. Waldorf Systems, which financed various vending machine companies, was in decline and, from Brody's point of view, derailed RA from its creative and glamorous path. Perhaps, the Wechslers felt that they could force their coffee into all their new vending machines. The nurture of their core coffee business struck closer to home than Brody's ambitions.

Slater and Martin Brody knew they would have to fold the operations of Waldorf into Brody's RA operations to make a half-decent balance sheet. They knew that Brody would never agree to such a thing. To force Brody out, the Wechslers would have to convince Grace to vote her 42% of the RA stock with the family and against Brody's 10%. That is what she did. In October 1963, Brody was forced to resign

Shortly thereafter, Waldorf, which had shown a net loss of more than a half million dollars the year before, announced its plans to acquire the outstanding shares of RA owned by the Wechsler family. A declining business had been allowed to swallow up a vital, growing one with great upward potential.

When news of Brody's ouster became known at Time-Life, the management and design contract for Le Western in Paris was abandoned. Brody's concept and design would later be acquired by Hilton Hotels, who, as previously stated, would use it in their Paris Hilton Le Western.

The previous owners of Divonne, realizing finally what the

construction of the new Geneva-Lausanne superhighway would mean to business, tried to buy the property back, offering RA $250,000 more than they had sold it for the previous year. But Wechsler turned them down. Ironically, Brody's partner in Divonne, Jean Claude Aaron of CFGHI led Abe Wechsler to an acceptable buyer, when he had introduced Wechsler to Eli de Rothschild during one of Wechsler's stays in Paris. At the same board meeting of RA at which Brody was dismissed, RA sold the Divonne property to Eli de Rothschild, who was in fact bidding on the property as the nominee of Jean Claude Aaron.

Through the Paris office of Cleary Gottlieb, the previous owners of Divonne made a higher bid, but it was rejected. Perhaps the Rothschild bloodline was worth the difference between the lower and the higher bids. Aaron subsequently turned the Divonne property into a huge profit center.

The Wechslers had sold Divonne cheaply. Aside from its profitability and cash flow, the French held all money re-invested in the hotel business tax-free.

The Jerome Brody era at Restaurant Associates had ended— just in time for his new life to begin.

Marlene

That Marlene Gray would become the office manager of CFGHI at the time of the RA purchase of Divonne-les-Bains was an unlikely occurrence. Marlene, who had lived in Paris for nine years, was a graduate of the Ecole d'Interprétes of the University of Geneva; fluent in German, Spanish, Italian, French and English, she was one of twenty-seven students out of 400 who had emerged successfully from the program. Her goal was to serve as a United Nations interpreter. If language was her most obvious vocational skill, her personal passion lay in the film world and the world of literature.

During her working years in France, Marlene was to assist on many international film co-productions with such filmmakers as Raoul Levy, Peter Rathvon, Jean Renoir, Peter Glenvill, and Harry Kurnitz, who wrote the screenplays for "On the Waterfront" and "The African Queen."

Marlene was born in Sumatra in 1931, where her father was in charge of a sisal plantation. Her mother came from a devout Roman Catholic family of ten. Her grandfather had married twice; his first wife gave him two boys, and when he remarried after her death, he had ten more children, all brought up in the Roman

Catholic Church.

Her grandfather was the owner, with his brother, of a large and successful Swiss embroidery business in St. Gallen, but none of his children, despite his eagerness to provide them with the best university education, would enter the family business.

When Marlene's mother married a Protestant, it scandalized her family and formented bitterness on both sides. The marriage was soon in trouble. In 1932, Marlene's father moved them to Ceylon where he became manager of a coconut plantation. They arrived on Marlene's first birthday. Her mother, trapped in a marriage kept together only by her Roman Catholic avoidance of divorce, decided that Marlene needed a superior education. In addition to that concern, she wanted to remove her from the malarial climate of the plantation.

The boarding school Marlene attended from the age of 5, until after the War when she was 14, was the Good Shepherd Convent, high in the drier, cooler mountains at Nuwara Eliya. Here she thrived and studied a classic curriculum, which included Latin. Marlene loved the school, which many other plantation students attended. Her Irish missionary nuns were totally dedicated. She had a full spectrum of classes—geography, music, botany—but her favorites were literature and the theater. She was a natural athlete, played field hockey, was captain of the netball team (a version of basketball), and roller-skated. Her strong imagination and sense of self flourished within the limits set by her school.

When she returned for visits to the plantation, she found a large porched colonial with shadowy verandahs and a quiet library to browse in and to dream the dreams of "Treasure Island" and "Gone with the Wind." For Marlene, it was a world of books and pet animals, including her own Arabian horse, "Rajah."

But while life passed pleasantly and productively for young

Marlene, her mother was having a tougher time. Eventually, after both of her own parents died, despite the reservations of her Catholicism, she divorced, when Marlene was 14.

At the end of World War II, as soon as she could, Marlene's mother took Marlene and her brother, John, now seven years old, back to school in Switzerland. She then returned to Ceylon to marry Robbie Gray in 1947. Robbie Gray had been an acquaintance of many years and managed a tea plantation upcountry in the so-called Uva Highlands in Ceylon. After four years at the *Institut du Sacre Coeur* in Estavayer-le-lac, Marlene, now 18, once again returned to the plantation.

When she returned, life with her mother and stepfather seemed luxurious, a soothing contrast to the rigors of a sensible Catholic boarding school. Ceylon became a magical place for her. She remembers her stepfather's reflecting on their bounteous isolation. For him Ceylon had become "a fool's paradise," implying that the end of colonialism would herald their expulsion from Eden.

The 6000-acre estate was called Attampettia, and on it, the Grays made their own bread and butter, bred pigs, grew vegetables, etc. The only things they bought were fish, flour, and wines. Her mother was in charge of the gardens. Help in Ceylon was abundant. One day, while inspecting the tea estate with her Papa, after a disagreement with her mother, he took some of the rain-moist, red earth into his hands and bade her smell its freshness. He said: "Whatever happens, you will always have the earth."

Privileged to have had her glimpse of paradise and to feel her spirit soar within it, young Marlene had also lived and learned in Switzerland, in a world where the rules of life were strict and where one got only what one earned. Many years later, when she and Jerry Brody bought their first home in Columbia County,

New York, it was, for her, a reunion with the soil from which she had drawn such sustenance.

Robbie Gray took over the responsibility of paying for the children's education. Marlene had developed ambitions to be a dancer or actress, but tempering romance with caution, she accepted her mother's and stepfather's advice and did the business school version of the baccalaureate. She also learned accounting and shorthand. Her facility with languages led her to study at the University of Geneva.

While at the university, Marlene set out to master Spanish. Since she believed that the fastest way to do that was total immersion, she asked her mother to send her off to Spain, where she would live with a German couple living in Madrid. Spirited, attractive, and filled with energy, style, and curiosity, Marlene viewed Spain as a working holiday.

In Madrid, Marlene became the secretary to Tim Healy of the Motion Picture Association of America. Marlene told her mother that she planned to vacation in Seville during Holy Week. Charles Bailey, a successful publisher from Chicago, had been visiting the Grays in Ceylon, and Marlene's mother told her that she had instructed him to deliver a gift to her in Seville, where he too planned to spend Holy Week.

In order to deliver the gift, Bailey invited Marlene to come to his hotel. They had tea. He then encouraged her to join him for dinner to meet his good friends Lillian Gish and John and Elaine Steinbeck, who were on their honeymoon. Dinner was a great success.

The Steinbecks and Bailey offered to drive Marlene back to Madrid, and by the time they bid one another farewell, they vowed to keep in touch. Steinbeck offered to use his influence at his alma mater, Stanford University, to get Marlene a scholarship.

Marlene eventually returned to Geneva with her Spanish language credits to resume her studies. She was amazed and delighted when she received news from Stanford that she had gotten the scholarship. Marlene immediately cabled her parents in Ceylon, only to have to tell them three weeks later that Stanford had re-wired to report that the acceptance had been a mistake. Steinbeck was infuriated. It took 3 years of investigation before he discovered that a member of the Stanford admissions committee had learned that Marlene's candidacy had been backed by Steinbeck whose name appeared on the Hollywood "Gray List" as a person with un-American leanings. The bite of the McCarthy Era was deep and poisonous.

Despite the loss of the opportunity to come to America to study—Marlene had a strong desire to see America, matched only by her desire to see Russia—her friendship with Steinbeck paid off. Steinbeck, who had been commissioned to write several articles by *Le Figaro Littéraire*, hired Marlene, upon her graduation, to work for him during his Paris sojourn. It is a sad indication of the repression of the McCarthy era that one of Marlene's duties was to deliver Steinbeck's articles to James Brady at the American Embassy so that they could be vetted for political correctness.

Marlene, with the support of the Steinbecks, remained active in the film industry, and it was in this period that her life was vitalized by contact with some of Europe's best filmmakers.

It was from out of the blue that Marlene was asked by Jean François Rozan, her professor at the Ecole d' Interprétes and now partner of SEFRI, to become the executive secretary to Germain Vidal, president of CFGHI. Her language skills would be of great value to him.

Since one of the first requirements for the job was to travel to America with the Vidals to visit hotel and casino venues in the United States and Puerto Rico, Marlene could satisfy her desire to see America. At Orly airport, Marlene ate what she thought would be her last satisfactory croissant and sipped her last French expresso. Boarding the plane at the last possible moment, she joined the Vidals and the three began their first journey to America.

Vidal was pleasantly surprised when Brody, looking handsome and confident as usual, personally met them at the airport; they were taken by limousine to a large suite in the Waldorf. That night, the Brodys, the Lewises, and the Baums joined Marlene and the Vidals at the Four Seasons, then in the full flush of its renown. Marlene, who was awestruck by the energy and scope of New York, nonetheless kept her critical faculties intact; she remembers wondering why such a beautiful restaurant would be so dark that it was impossible to see the food and thought it odd that breakfast croissants would be served with dinner.

The next morning, Marlene and the Vidals reported to the West 57th Street headquarters of Restaurant Associates to begin their indoctrination. Vidal, who spoke or understood little English, probably learned very little. But that was all right, since his job was essentially to peddle influence among the French "old boys."

Marlene could not help but be favorably impressed by the loyalty and devotion of Brody's entire staff, which treated him like a hero, as if their well-being depended in large part on his abilities and decency. In fact, Brody had initiated a stock-sharing plan with the employees, which had done much to insure his popularity.

The Dorado Beach Hotel and Casino in Puerto Rico, owned by the Rockefellers, were next on the itinerary, and then Miami, Los Angeles and the Beverly Hills Hotel, and then on to Las

Vegas. Compared with the relative austerity of post-War Europe, the America to which Marlene was first exposed seemed impressively vigorous. The Dorado Beach, the Four Seasons and the Beverly Hills Hotel fared well in comparison with most of their peers around the world. By the time the entourage arrived in Las Vegas, Marlene was overwhelmed.

In those days in Las Vegas, people dressed for dinner and the entertainment, and the gambling was restricted to the main rooms of the casinos, without the omnipresent sprawl of today's slot machines or the racket and incivility of the *hoi polloi*.

Marlene liked Las Vegas and she was about to be offered a once-in-a-lifetime treat. Alan Lewis called Marlene's room and asked her if she wanted to join him and the Vidals to see Frank Sinatra's one-man show. Not only did she get to see Sinatra, but that night, Sammy Davis, Jr. and Dean Martin joined him for a full-blown performance of "The Rat Pack." Marlene had finally seen America, and she had been delighted.

Once back in Paris, Marlene learned that Brody had decided to develop Divonne-les-Bains as a corporate convention center, a concept that was then alien to Europe. Marlene's major task became drumming up business among the European corporate elite. In fact, she was out of the office so much, she had to hire a secretary to handle routine matters.

The French partners were pleased with Marlene's growing involvement in CFGHI. Not only was she instrumental in developing the Brody-inspired corporate conference business, but she was the woman on-the-spot whenever they or Brody dispatched a VIP to Divonne for the red carpet treatment. They considered her one of them, meaning "French," unlike Brody, who was not.

In the mind of her friend, Jean François Rozan, she had become so much a part of the French team that he invited

Marlene to a lunch and decided to share with her an important and sensitive bit of information. She listened with carefully guarded amazement as Rozan told her that his French partners were planning to force Brody out. After all they were the ones who had raised the $3 million. And, of course, Brody was not part of their "old boy" network.

Jean François Rozan could not have guessed Marlene's reaction. She asked herself a basic question: Who was paying her salary. The answer was Brody.

She wrote a long letter to Brody, who, when he received it, called her immediately and said he would be in Paris on the next possible flight. When Marlene arrived at the office at 10:00 AM, the hour that many Parisians call the start of the working day, Brody was already outside the office pacing. It is characteristic of him but surprising to those who do not know him well, that while he considered the matter crucial, he treated it coolly, without temper. Assessing the self-seeking "cliqueishness," which he knew from the outset characterized his partners, he left indignation aside. For the time being, he would do nothing but keep a sharp eye.

Brody's separation from Grace was progressing by slow degrees into a final divorce decree, but would be more than a year in finalization. The usual business demanded that Brody be in New York, as well as the extraordinary business in which he and Carl Hess were engaged—the raising of money to buy out the Wechslers. Divonne-les-Bains business also required Brody to make several trips to Paris, where, finally, he and Marlene Gray fell in love and committed themselves to one another.

Marlene was willing to live with Brody; Brody wanted to marry Marlene. But the separation agreement dragged on. When Marlene was offered an opportunity to work on a film project that would take five months of her time, the emotional issue came to a head. Marlene resigned from CFGHI, and on July 4, 1962, arrived in New York City in time for lunch with Brody at Lindy's with the largest strawberry shortcake she had ever seen.

Despite their being together and despite the fact that for both of them their love would become the profoundest and steadiest thing in their lives, it was especially difficult for Brody to be living with Marlene before the divorce decree became final. For Marlene, too, the issue of Brody's children was an emotional burden; she could put herself in their places. She too had been a child of divorce.

Brody took a separate studio apartment for Marlene, while in fact they lived together in Brody's Lexington Avenue bachelor apartment. In addition to the uncertainties of their situation, Brody had to bear up under the hostility of the Wechsler family and the bewilderment of his children. For the Brody children, the divorce had been devastating. Since the troubled marriage between Brody and Grace had not shown itself in overt ways, the children could not understand what had happened. They adored their father who they remembered as being at the center of fun. They traveled together to Mexico and Europe, they sailed, and Brody always made sure there was room enough for their friends. He had talked to them about his business with pride and they had heard from their friends that their father had made great successes in the business world. In the aftermath of the divorce, Kathy remembers sitting at the dinner table with her mother and her grandparents knowing that they were the people who were willing to ruin her father.

The ouster from RA in October had tightened the financial screws, so that Brody had to wonder how they expected him to make support payments while at the same time they took away his livelihood. Grace insisted that she would not grant Brody a divorce until she was certain that she had a new husband.

Fortunately, for all concerned, Grace found her man, and in the spring, immediately after the divorce decree became final, Marlene and Brody were married in a civil ceremony. Grace was married shortly thereafter.

Marlene traveled all over the city in the tow of real estate agents looking for a suitable apartment. Finally, the couple struck gold. Brody found a magnificent two-bedroom apartment high above Central Park South, with wraparound windows, commanding perfect views of the entire park.

Life after RA was just starting. Gallagher's, the Rainbow Room, L'Étoile, the Sherry Netherland, Raffles and the Ground Floor would take Brody back into the heart of the restaurant business, eventually yielding financial success greater than that of the days of RA and contentment he had never dreamed existed.

Gallagher's

This is a real New York joint—
Liza Minelli.

Brody grew tired of being out of the restaurant business in about two months. Invigorated by Carl Hess's prodding, Brody entered into negotiations to buy Jack Solomon's 1927 New York landmark steak house, Gallagher's, which he had come into when he married its owner, Helen Gallagher. While still with RA, Brody had unsuccessfully tried to buy the restaurant, but now, with Jack Solomon recently deceased and the restaurant in serious decline, it was a buyers' market. Despite the drawback of a short lease and a moribund business, Brody bought Gallagher's for $325,000, with $100,000 in cash borrowed from Abraham Claude, Jr. of the Morgan Guaranty Trust Company. The balance was to be paid in installments to Irene Hayes, Solomon's widow. Claude did not want Brody's RA stock as collateral. In fact, Claude insisted that Brody sell the stock. He would depend on Brody's talents to make good the loan even though Gallagher's gross income was down to about $750,000, compared with the $8.6 million it would grow to in the years following Brody's takeover.

The first days of the new regime were dismal. The restaurant needed everything from a good cleaning to a new clientele. The staff was dispirited. During Solomon's lengthy decline Gallagher's had lost its clout. Customers were so scarce that management hung a curtain between the bar room and the main dining room to disguise the big, empty spaces. The staff of waiters was down to six from sixteen. After 9:00 PM, only two waiters worked and the staff would lay green mats on the dining tables and play cards.

One of the first good omens was a visit paid to Brody by Toots Shor, the famous restaurant owner, man about town, and tippler. When Shor arrived at Gallagher's, he asked for Brody in order to wish him the best. Brody invited Toots to sit down and have a meal. Toots said he would rather sit at the bar. With his arm around Brody's shoulder, Toots called over the bartenders to whom he was a legend, and looking them menacingly in the eye said, "This guy is my friend, I want you to take good care of him." Brody had received the blessing of New York's most famous saloonkeeper. It was worth a lot.

Despite the hurdles the old restaurant had to overcome, Brody's fame among restaurateurs and clients was at its peak. The week that news of Brody's purchase of Gallagher's became public, dozens of congratulatory letters and telegrams poured in. One pleased Brody the most. He keeps it in his Central Park South apartment to this day.

Mr. J. Brody
I AM SENDIN YOU THIS NOTE CARE OF GALLAGHER'S, IN HOPES THAT YOU WILL RECEIVE IT.

I BOUGHT RA STOCK BECAUSE PEOPLE TOLD ME YOU WERE THE SMARTEST RESTAURANT MAN AROUND. SO I WANT TO WISH YOU ALL THE LUCK IN THE WORLD IN YOUR VENTURE. I HOPE YOU GET TO BE SO BIG THAT YOU BUY OUT RA AND THEN MY STOCK WILL GO UP AGAIN.

AGAIN, GOOD LUCK
Frances Smith

P.S. I'M INTERESTED INKNOWING IF YOU HAVE
STOCK OUT ON YOUR NEW BUSINESS.

Frances Smith's hope that Brody would grow big again was
to come true. Although, Brody never made his United Brody
Corp. restaurant properties a part of a public offering, he was
dreaming large dreams again, almost from the moment he took
over Gallagher's. Multi-restaurant schemes occurred to him like
dreams—not always good ones.

A month after the Gallagher purchase, that harbinger of good
news, Gus Eyssell, met with Brody at Gallagher's and asked him
to take over the management of the Rainbow Room in
Rockefeller Center, on terms Brody found impossible to turn
down. The space had become unproductive, and Eyssell considered Brody the most creative restaurant entrepreneur in the fine
dining industry. A deal was struck in which Brody would take a
10-year lease and pay 6% on the first one million of gross
income. Eyssell offered to stop all further payments at the
million dollar ceiling, but Brody *talked him into* taking 2% above
a million.

The Rainbow Room, situated on the 65th floor of the RCA
building in Rockefeller Center, has the most spectacular view of
midtown Manhattan. It was founded in 1934, and had featured
the big band of Ray Noble, Edgar Bergen and Charley McCarthy,
the Glen Gray Orchestra, the Pickens Sisters, Judy Holliday and
Mary Martin. The Rainbow Room was credited with populariz-
ing waltz contests and the Big Apple in the 1930s. But when the
War came, the entire operation was closed down and not
re-opened until October 1950 when Union News Company

re-opened the big room and ran it as a luncheon club. An attempt was made to remodel the room and run it once again as a dinner club, but by 1964 Rockefeller Center officials announced that Union News's lease had been terminated by mutual consent. When Brody agreed to take on the management of the Rainbow Room, Gus Eyssell's news release read, "It is hoped the fresh concepts of the new management will create a restaurant of unexcelled quality."

The undertaking was a huge one. Brody would move his chief chef, Fred Platzner, from Gallagher's to become chief chef of the Rainbow Room. His domain would include 400 seats in the room and the grill, another 100 in the cocktail lounges adjoining the room and about 400 more diners in the 64th floor private dining rooms. Brody would also provide cooking and table service for the 1,100 members of the Rockefeller Center Luncheon Club.

Brody's comment at the time was that he did not consider entertainment as too likely an item on his Rainbow Room menu. The emphasis would be on food. Unfortunately, in the first days of the new management, the most notable thing about the Rainbow Room were the empty tables.

The event, which gave the greatest impetus to the new, success of the enterprise, occurred about three months after Brody had taken over the Rainbow Room. At a menu meeting of his staff, Brody announced that the Rainbow Room would be hosting a dinner gala to celebrate the opening of a new Broadway play, "Funny Girl," starring Barbra Streisand. Brody made it clear that a perfunctory menu would not do if the Rainbow Room was to establish itself as a premier dining spot. Brody suggested what he thought would be the *piéce de résistance*, perfectly prepared pommes soufflées. Chef Max Putier, loved the idea. He was proud of his pommes soufflées. Then Brody told him that he would be preparing pommes soufflées for 400 people. Putier was aghast.

Max Putier had recently come to work at the Rainbow Room under the direction of head chef Fred Platzner. Putier was himself a world-class chef, who had been trained under such culinary talents as chef-owner Fernand Point of La Pyramide. Putier measured his skills by the most exacting standards of French *haute cuisine*. He and Platzner were destined to cross swords.

Putier had a passionate Gallic temperament that suffused his whole soul. His heavily French-accented English rose easily to enthusiasms and hardened bitterly over antagonisms. He had near zero tolerance for compromise and a strong conviction that his understanding of *haute cuisine* and kitchen management were the right ones.

The year was 1967, and Putier, who had just been promoted to executive chef, had hired three young chefs from Chez Bardet in Montreal, who had been trained in the Plaza Athenée in Paris. Putier thought they were young geniuses, and he commandeered their services for the pommes soufflées tasting, but even they became tentative when they learned that they would be preparing pommes soufflées for 400.

Putier joined chefs Girard, Andre and Pascal on the front lines and told them that they would each have to peel the potatoes. He could not accept the risk of less excellent chefs damaging a potato. Two chefs peeled, one chef sliced, one chef cooked the slices in hot oil twice—the first time at medium heat to put a water-resistant crust on the potato—the second time at high heat to puff out the potato slice with the expanding vapor. By the time the evening of the gala arrived, Putier had been screaming so much that he had lost his voice and had to give instructions by writing them on a piece of paper.

The "Funny Girl" dinner gathered enormous publicity and praise for the Rainbow Room. The next Saturday night, Brody, who was used to looking at elaborately set empty tables, looked at a full house. The *Holiday* Magazine plaque commemorating the excellence of the dinner hung in the Rainbow Room for 30 years.

Only two weeks later, the Rainbow Room hosted a similar opening night dinner party for Richard Burton's modern-dress "Hamlet." Whatever importance Burton's genius lent to the dramatic theater, the appearance of his new wife, Elizabeth Taylor, managed to overshadow it. Once again, the theater dinner party cast the flattering glow of celebrity on the Rainbow Room, and the food, service, view, and ambiance did the rest.

While business at the Rainbow Room blossomed, the Rainbow Grill, newly conceived and designed by Brody, languished. One evening Brody grimly eyed the empty tables. He went over to the New York phone book, and looked up the telephone number of the clarinet player Benny Goodman. Brody asked Goodman to play the Rainbow Grill; the notoriously stingy Goodman, pleased by the opportunity to be in on the beginning of a new venture and delighted not to pay a percentage to his booking agent, said he would.

Laurence Rockefeller, whose offices were on the 56th floor of Rockefeller Center, was so proud of the Benny Goodman booking, he demanded that his staff attend the show. Rockefeller's pride in the re-invigorated Rainbow Room and the excitement of the Grill was evident during Brody's entire lease.

Under the guidance of Tony Cabot, who would lead the musical operations in addition to his own renowned dance band, the Rainbow Grill moved into high gear. In the coming years, great musicians and singers, including Duke Ellington, Ella Fitzgerald, Dudley Moore, Peggy Lee, and Cleo Lane (now Dame) and John Dankworth, would make the Rainbow Grill a top attraction.

However, after ten years of the Rainbow Room and the Grill's contributing to the rental attractiveness of the RCA building, and with the departure of Gus Eyssell, the renewal lease offered to Brody was prohibitively expensive. When Brody announced that he would leave, Laurence Rockefeller did nothing to intercede.

In the next few years, as his success grew, Brody would experience mixed emotions seeing his grand RA creations, now under the control of the hostile element that had opposed him, in decline or shuttered. Divonne-les-Bains was sold off almost immediately, Time-Life pulled out of Le Western, the lease on La Fonda del Sol was sold to a bank, and the Forum of the Twelve Caesars became an Indian restaurant. Even the Four Seasons, saddled with mediocrity that Joe Baum could not alleviate, did not shine again until Kovi and Margatai, who had bought it from RA, were out from under the Restaurant Associates team headed by Martin Brody.

Whatever the loss of his RA creations may have caused Brody in regrets, it was not visible either in his demeanor or in his bottom line. In these years Gallagher's and the Rainbow Room and Grill would become enormous successes. Success bred an ambitious program of expansion, eventually to include L'Étoile, the Sherry Netherland, Raffles, the Grand Central Oyster Bar and the Ground Floor.

But in 1964, Brody's first task was to bring Gallagher's back to life. He never doubted Gallagher's for a moment. That a decade later, some of the other restaurant ventures would bring the United Brody Corp. to the brink of bankruptcy he had as yet no inkling.

Brody's belief in Gallagher's had to do with its authenticity. It had its own New York history and nothing could take that away. You could not start a place like Gallagher's; you had to acquire it. When you're in Gallagher's, you have no doubt where you are. As Bryan Reidy, its present manager says, "this place has an attitude."

Gallagher's had started life as a speakeasy in 1927, owned by Helen Gallagher, a Ziegfield Girl from the Follies. Helen and Jack turned Gallagher's into a steak house, building the two open brick charcoal ovens, and barbecuing steaks from the best prime meat available. When Helen Gallagher died, Jack married Irene Hayes, who was a partner in the famous florists, Irene Hayes, Wadley Smythe, and remained Solomon's active partner in the restaurant up to the day of his death.

At the foyer entrance to Gallagher's, there has always stood a room-sized, glass-sided meat locker, in which, stacked on butcher blocks, are sides of the finest slowly aging prime meat in the world. For the masculine appetites of Gallagher's regulars, that meat locker has always been a gourmand's peep show.

Helen, the Follies girl, and Jack, the bookie, attracted a colorful crowd, and everyone who was anyone in New York hung out at the bar, including mayor Jimmy Walker, most of the city's bigtime mobsters, bookies, stars of the theater world, and athletes and their adoring fans from Madison Square Garden, just down the street.

When Broadway had eighty shows running and the longest runs were under a year, Gallagher's was a prime theater hangout, recycling the theater-goers who had something new to see each month. Added to the mix were European tourists making Gallagher's an international destination. That Helen Gallagher's girl friends were beautiful Follies girls whose patronage created a wake of well-healed male admirers was good for business, also.

Even today, the walls at Gallagher's are covered with hundreds of photographs of New Yorkers from the Roaring '20s and before: men in stiff collars and bowler hats, gentlemen and elaborately dressed ladies out for a day at the track, and boxing champions, such as the picture of the sweltering 1934 press party held for Max Baer at Gallagher's. Pictures of stars of the silent screen, such as Mary Pickford, horse portraits of the great thoroughbred bloodlines, art nouveau covers of the pre-Playbill theater magazine "The Theatre," and an extravagant collection of signed major league baseball photographs, rare, nostalgic, and invaluable vie with each other for wall space. New Yorkers, especially the "pub jockeys," whose memories of the good times at Gallagher's were fading, needed only the announcement of Brody's purchase to be ready to renew old loyalties.

In fact, the restaurant began to do good business amazingly quickly. The *New York Times* had featured the fact that Brody had bought Gallagher's shortly after his divorce. Almost immediately divorced men and their girlfriends formed a new Gallagher's clique. The "king of the bookies" told Brody that he would guarantee that all his clients would be urged to honor good old Gallagher's and the horse crowd, sensing the new action, soon crowded round the bar as in days of yore.

Gallagher's was going full steam ahead, and it was impossible for Brody to manage both the Rainbow Room and Gallagher's. Enter Richard Conlon.

Dick Conlon had been with the Playboy Club, when it was at its swinging, hedonistic, sporting-life peak. Conlon himself was a tremendous, roaring character. He would hang around the bar, cocktail in hand, and tell stories all night or until the last customer went home. He was a great mingler, who knew the restaurant and professional sporting crowd well. Of the saints and sinners who populate the world, he was best acquainted with the latter, and one could feel reassured that Conlon had personal identification with most of transgressions of his regular crowd, who took him, therefore, to be one of their own.

Conlon attracted a number of famous professional athletes

to Gallagher's and these athletes in turn attracted the New York jock watchers. Joe DiMaggio, Joe Namath, Frank Gifford, and Kyle Rote became business-building attractions. During the week before their heavyweight championship bout at the Garden, and on the same night Mohammed Ali and George Foreman dined at Gallagher's.

Eventually, Conlon would have to choose between the athletes and the bookies, as the czars of professional sports and the FBI were made anxious by the fraternization of sports heroes and bookies. The bookies, no matter their past loyalties to Gallagher's and Jack Solomon, its bookie founder, were made unwelcome.

That Giant owner Wellington Mara was a betting man himself made the path to Gallagher's doorstep even more convivial for team loyalists. In conjunction with New York Giant defensive lineman Tom Scott, Conlon formed the "Kickoff Club," which was a series of lunches for Giants' season ticket holders where they would meet the players and coaches with no press around to hinder candor. This strategic move to bring in the Giants fans broadened to include all of New York's major league sports teams.

Gallagher's 52nd prospered as never before. Conlon's charm cast a net wider than just to sports. Jackie Onassis, Anthony Quinn, and Richard Burton were regulars. Marilyn Monroe and her super agent, John Springer, often dined at Gallagher's; Conlon showed her the large, framed photograph of Joe DiMaggio, which "The Yankee Clipper" had autographed for Brody. One night after dinner at Gallagher's, Princess Grace asked Conlon to have Gallagher's cater the July 4, 1966 barbecue she was hosting in Monaco at the Golf of Mont-Agel. The entrée was "Prime Black Angus Charcoal Broiled Steak," the tossed salad was dressed with Gallagher's house dressing, the tomatoes were from New Jersey, the dessert strawberries from California, and the apple pie from

Washington state. The menu credit read "This menu has been prepared by: GALLAGHER'S NEW YORK'S OFFICIAL STEAK HOUSE."

No matter how successfully Conlon and, later on, subsequent managers were running Gallagher's, Brody remained a regular on-site presence. He recognized that Gallagher's had developed an historic reputation as a great steak house in a one-of-a-kind ambiance. During one severe meat shortage, the price of prime beef shot up seventy percent. Brody's manager was distressed at the price he had to report to Brody, but he need not have been. Tomatoes went from $9/case to $60. Brody told his manager that they wouldn't stay at $60 forever. They didn't call it a "Steak House Tomato" for nothing.

The same ruled applied when the antiquated air-conditioning system was on the brink of failure. It could be patched for $6,000 or replaced for $30,000. Again, for Brody, there was no question whether they should spend the money to safeguard the equity of the Gallagher's name.

Like Mama Leone's, Gallagher's was a landmark. The lesson Brody learned from the enormous success of Mama Leone's stood him in good stead at Gallagher's. Later on, having resurrected one dinosaur, he was confident that he could resurrect another at the Grand Central Oyster Bar.

These restaurants did not to need to be remodeled every five years, to depend on the whims of the latest food critic, or on expensively contrived promotions to attract a new client base. Gallagher's and the Oyster Bar weathered the hard times of the 1970s because their loyal customers made them the last cut when discretionary dollars got leaner. Even when Raffles, L'Étoile, and the Café Bar at the Sherry Netherland were bringing Brody to the edge of bankruptcy, he was buying $60 crates of tomatoes for Gallagher's.

These landmarks endure and have spun off a considerable fortune, while the more faddish ventures, after flashy starts, did not survive.

At The End of
The Rainbow

If the newly married Brodys had needed a lot of leisure time together in order to solidify their new lives, they would have been sadly disappointed. When Brody became the owner of Gallagher's, he also became its full-time manager. When Brody found Dick Conlon to replace him as manager of Gallagher's, he immediately became the full-time manager of the even more time-consuming Rainbow Room. Brody's days started before the luncheon crowd arrived and ended in the wee hours of the morning when the last Grill Room customers wrapped up their night's revelry.

Marlene would visit Jerry at the Rainbow Room and then at the other restaurants that he either managed or owned. Except for weekends their time together was limited. When the stressful last days of the Sherry Netherland enterprises were exhausting them both, a country retreat appealed to them more strongly than ever before.

In the first years of their marriage Marlene had the support and companionship of some of her best friends from her days in Europe and Asia. When she was a young girl in Ceylon, her parents had become friends of the Ondaatje family whose son

Michael would develop into the world-renowned poet and novelist, best known for "The English Patient." Now that Michael and his wife were living in Toronto, there were frequent occasions to get together in New York. Marlene drew great sustenance from Ondaatje's artistic genius and humanity. Elaine and John Steinbeck were back in New York and that friendship too ripened, enabling Marlene to give to Brody the gift of her friendships and interests in the world of art and culture.

While working in Paris, Marlene had met John Lefebre, his wife Ljuba and young daughter Marion. Originally from Berlin, Germany, John worked for MGM. In 1936, Culture Minister Goebels demanded that he and his family leave Germany. They fled to the United States. By the time Marlene met the Lefebres, John worked for 20th Century Fox, which sent the family to Egypt and then to Paris where he was in charge of distribution for the Middle East. In 1960, John, realized a long-nurtured dream: to open his own art gallery in New York. Over the years John had collected the work of young artists, whom he could afford. He became the supporter of many from the COBRA movement.

In large part through his mentoring, the Brodys began to develop a collection of distinction and value. It is unlikely that, without Marlene's commitment to art and her friends in the art world, Brody would have the opportunity to discover and develop his own devotion to collecting.

Featured in Lefebre's collection was the work of Pierre Alechinsky which the Brodys started to collect and with whom they became lifelong friends. In 1998, in a culmination of their devotion to the man and his work, several masterpieces from the Brodys' collection of Alechinskys, which hung in their Central Park South apartment, were chosen by the Jeu de Paume to be exhibited at Alechinsky's show in Paris.

The Onaatjes, the Steinbecks, the Lefebres and Alechinskys

enriched the Brodys' lives at a time when the demands of business, Marlene's acclimatization to her new country, Brody's distance from his children, the hard times of L'Étoile, and the Sherry Netherland misfortunes would otherwise had made life a harsher proposition.

Brody, too, found comfort and warmth with friends who would remain close to him: Carl Hess, his brilliant financial consultant, and his wife Desa; Rudy deHarak, the graphics designer; Allen Grover of Time-Inc.; John Springer; and Allston Boyer, the patrician ally of Lawrence Rockefeller.

But the commitment to manage his restaurant business and to expand it was at the center of Brody's life: Social and artistic respites were just that—welcome, but occasional, resting spots during the hectic days of business.

The idea of creating the Rainbow Grill as a cocktail lounge and musical entertainment center to complement the more formal Rainbow Room was Brody's. In order to distinguish the ambiance of the Rainbow Grill from the spacious grandeur of the Rainbow Room, Brody planned to lower the ceilings or, as is still in debate, raise the floors. Officials of Rockefeller Center objected, claiming that the new floor levels would slice across the otherwise homogeneous window heights of the other sixty-four floors of the RCA Building. When it finally became clear that from the street level the spacing of the windows on the 65th floor would be visible to no one, the Brody re-design was allowed to proceed. The Rainbow Grill became one of the most stylish and luxurious cocktail lounges in the world, offering a blend of intimacy and spaciousness, of elegance and comfort that is always felt anew.

In 1966, Brody aggressively began to upgrade the reputation of the cuisine at the Rainbow Room by sponsoring such events as a dinner series given by the *Confrerie de la Chaine des Rotisseurs*, the oldest gourmet society in the world. The pinnacle of culinary excellence in the Rainbow Room was achieved in 1968 when Christian Millau (of the famous international guide team, Gault-Millau), who was a lifelong friend, organized an event in which Paul Bocuse used the kitchens of the Rainbow Room to create masterpieces of French cuisine using ingredients entirely native to America. The experiment received enormous press coverage and raised the expectations of dining at the Rainbow Room to gourmet standards.

Brody instituted what became the famous "Fortnights," at which a cuisine of one nation was featured: English, Greek, Spanish, and Italian. They became sellouts.

Along with the success of musical headline entertainment and world-class cuisine, Brody used Earl Blackwell to assemble the most glittery names of the Celebrity Register to attend what would become the socially coveted "Nine O'Clocks" at the Rainbow Room. Blackwell started the "Nine O'Clocks" in 1964. Three or four parties were organized each year. "Suzy Knickerbocker" raved about this "glamorous new group and its formidable board of governors" which included: Mrs. Lyon Slater, Mr. and Mrs. Kingman Douglas, Mr. and Mrs. James Van Alen, Mrs. William Langley, Mr. and Mrs. Frederick Brisson, Earl Blackwell, Mr. and Mrs. John R. Drexel III, Mr. & Mrs. Zachary Scott, Miss Anita Colby, Mrs. Albert Lasker, Mr. Lauder Greenway, Col. Serge Obolensky and Milton Holden. It was Blackwell's gathering up of the hard-core Newport-New York social group, the inner circle.

And so to all its other virtues, the Rainbow Room added the social hype of the in-crowd, a crowd to whom Jerry Brody never was and has never been attracted. When asked in 1970 about his reaction to the Rainbow Room Nine O'Clocks, Brody replied, "They were just sort of friendly things." His ingenuousness, either feigned or real, would not protect him from social climbers and elitists—as his continued association with Blackwell's in-crowd would show him first hand during the heyday of Raffles.

With Gallagher's business booming and with the Rainbow Room matching its success and celebrity, Brody needed managers he could depend on to give him time for other projects. Bryan Daley at the Rainbow Room, as Richard Conlon at Gallagher's, was just such a person.

Only three years after his uncivil ouster from RA, leaving an entire working life of achievement in the hands of people he did not respect, an undaunted Brody jumped back into business as the owner of Gallagher's, overseeing its celebrated re-emergence as a profitable enterprise. Almost simultaneously with the task of running, merchandising, and paying for Gallagher's, he had taken on the huge responsibility of revitalizing and managing the Rainbow Room. But even these hectic activities did not deter him from visions of expanding his restaurant domain. Determined to leave the debacle of RA in the rear-view mirror, he set off on a course to make the new United Brody Corp. New York's premier restaurant institution.

In 1966, when the funds to undertake such an enterprise with its own capital were unavailable, at the request of William S. Paley of CBS, the United Brody Corp. won the contract to manage the brand new and opulent Ground Floor restaurant in "Black Rock," CBS's corporate headquarters in Rockefeller Center. It was a temporary, stylish, and financially rewarding step towards ownership.

As one might have expected from the exacting Paley, who cared mightily about good food and aesthetics, the Ground Floor was to be a showpiece, with no expense, either cash or talent, to be spared. For talent, for Paley, Brody was the right man. The Four Seasons and La Fonda Del Sol were more than adequate proof of Brody's familiarity with the type of posh, dramatic elegance Paley wanted to create at the Ground Floor. Brody's general manager at the Ground Floor was the charming, hardworking, and financially astute Eivind Urbye, a Norwegian. He would become the manager at Raffles and, eventually, would have major success in the nightclub and restaurant industry in his native country, in whose enterprises Brody would become a partner.

It is remarkable how many formative elements the Ground Floor shared with the Four Seasons. It is most likely that Paley was aware of them all. The wealth of CBS and Paley paralleled the wealth of Seagram and Sam Bronfman, both of whom personally dominated corporations which would house restaurants intended to trumpet the pre-eminence of their corporate sponsors. The world-class architects of both the Seagram Building (Mies van de Rohe and Philip Johnson), and the CBS Headquarters (Eero Saarinen and Kevin Roche Associates) were approved by proprietors whose concern for design excellence and public affirmation of their superior taste was inseparable from their interest in the restaurant business. The exquisite and expensive attention to the interior appointments, which in the Four Seasons were masterminded by the Huxtables and in the Ground Floor by Warren Platzer of Eero Saarinen and Associates, further bespoke a commitment to elegance that was as much a personal requirement of their chiefs as it was a dispassionate financial and marketing strategy.

As befitted the monolithic power of the CBS building itself, unequivocal masculine strength was called for. As *Interior* magazine reported of Paley's goals: "a total abjuration of the phony; a menu both hearty and international; uncompromising quality in food, service, and decor, with commensurate prices; an open kitchen and stand-up bar; no aping of period decor, but traditional luxuries—fine mahogany, leather, velour, brass, crystal, silver, china; what *looked* expensive would be expensive."

The Ground Floor and the Four Seasons were justifiably admired showplaces, but Brody's association with the former, no matter what kind of favorable attention might be brought to it and to Brody himself, would lack the very same fulfillment as had the latter: pride of ownership and the satisfaction of control. Although, as Brody himself admits, until his in-laws dramatically proved otherwise, he had come to believe that the Four Seasons was, in fact, his and his alone. But Brody never fooled himself that the Ground Floor was anyone else's bailiwick but CBS's. While the limelight and the management fees associated with running the Ground Floor were important to Brody, what Brody was looking for was another great restaurant to call his own.

In much the same way that the brand new Seagram Building had made Brody think it would generate restaurant demand, so did the newly completed General Motors Headquarters building on 59th Street and Fifth Avenue. Brody's inquiries at the New York landmark Sherry Netherland Hotel, just across 59th Street from the General Motors Building, yielded the information that the business in the Sherry Netherland Cafe Restaurant needed improvement, that the room service contract, now being inadequately handled by the Sherry Netherland's co-op was available, and that a basement room in the hotel was available and could be used for a dining club and disco. Additional space in the Sherry Netherland was available for a major luxury restaurant. With the help of a $2 million unsecured loan from the SBIC, which made the money available to Brody on the strength of his reputation and track record, Brody took advantage of the opportunities the Sherry Netherland offered.

In large part inspired by his wife Marlene's vision of bringing an essentially Parisian restaurant to New York, Brody became the owner and the creator of the Alexander Girard-designed *L'Étoile*. Along with that undertaking, he would, in short order, take over the cafe at the Sherry Netherland, room service for the Sherry Netherland Hotel, and, in its basement create, along with Cecil Beaton, New York's most socially exclusive super club-nightclub-disco for the rich and the famous: Raffles.

L'Étoile

The landlords of The Newarker and the Hawaian Room had provided Brody with restaurant spaces which perfectly fitted his economic criteria of minimum upfront expenditure and who allowed his RA team to dictate their own design, levels of service, cuisine and marketing strategies. The advantage of Mama Leone's was that by the time Brody acquired it and its lease at a surprisingly low cost, it had become a New York destination restaurant and a full-blown cash cow. The Rainbow Room, although in serious decline, still had invaluable brand equity and unique physical beauty and was turned over to Brody on a utopian lease. Gallagher's, another landmark destination restaurant, needed only respect, faith, and intelligent management to restore it to full health. Perhaps, in the glow of all the positive elements connected with his new enterprises, Brody paid insufficient attention to the fact that in the three years since his ouster from Restaurant Associates, two of his RA showcase restaurants, the Forum of the Twelve Caesars and La Fonda del Sol, which had not benefited from cost-free start-ups and landmark status, were experiencing hard times. Even the uniquely splendid Four Seasons, much blessed by Seagram start up money and continued owner loyalty, was slumping under the heavy-handedness of the new RA, despite the best efforts of the brilliant Joe Baum. Undoubtedly contributing to their hard times was the unenlightened mediocrity of the new RA cadre, but perhaps there were larger, impersonal forces at work. Without the impetus of sweetheart landlord deals or the accumulated equity of landmark restaurants, it would not surprise any restaurant industry analyst to predict that the dark side of restaurant economics might revolve into a slumping phase—no matter who was running the show.

A large part of Brody's faith in the expansion of RA had been based on his vision of New York's robust, long-term economic growth, and in that climate of optimism and prosperity, the endemic risks of restaurant ownership might have submerged from view and consciousness.

Even as L'Étoile, Brody's wholly-owned new restaurant, opened its doors in the spring of 1966, its excellences were being touted in the food press. L'Étoile was meant to be pure French Parisian. Alvin Kerr, reviewing L'Étoile for *Gourmet* (September 1966) captured just how focused Brody and Marlene were on making L'Étoile a memorable bit of Paris in New York.

Early this summer there appeared on my desk a small tin, of the size usually associated with such comestibles as tomato paste and frozen concentrated fruit juice. Whence it came or by whose hand I had no idea, but it was obvious from its weight that the contents were not what the size of the can suggested. It was light as air—which, as I finally determined from the label, was exactly what it did contain—air of Paris. It was, the label assured me, absolutely genuine air, packed in Paris, and presumably, '*appellation controlée*,' to be used as needed to relieve depression brought on by too long an absence from the

City of Light. One had only to open the can, inhale the air, and *voilà, Paris!* I was awfully tempted to try it, but I really didn't need the air at that moment, having been in Paris not too long before, and it seemed a pity to waste it. I was away during August, and when I returned I found the tin already opened. The air was gone. In its place was a note. 'This was stale,' it read. 'For refreshing air of Paris visit the restaurant called **L'Étoile** at 1 East 59th Street.

Ironically, one of those lines of praise was a herald of why L'Étoile succeeded as a design and culinary concept yet could not stay the course as a business enterprise. Kerr wrote, "As a restaurant it is way ahead of its time...." Owning a restaurant that is way ahead of its time is similar to owning a stock that is way ahead of its time: the satisfactions, if any, are intellectual rather than financial.

The waiters at L'Étoile addressed their customers in French, unless spoken to in English. For any non-French speaker who has been made to feel like a cultural yahoo by a disdainful Frenchman, such Parisian authenticity is a qualified virtue— but Brody was counting on there being enough New Yorkers sufficiently urbane to require a true Parisian culinary experience, and that their numbers would create a viable client base. In any game plan based on the assumption of relatively rapid economic growth, it is important to recognize that a significant percentage of the restaurant population would come from new money, who require an education in good food. They would have to go to culinary highschool before they could attend Harvard. L'Étoile was Harvard.

Brody made Max Putier, whose culinary ambitions were inspired by the high standards Brody had set for L'Étoile, the chief chef. Putier had first gone to work for Brody at the

Rainbow Room, working under Fred Platzner whom Putier quickly came to dislike. Within the first month of his employment at the Rainbow Room, Putier concluded that he could not work under Platzner, and, despite the great respect, indeed awe, which Putier had for Brody he abruptly resigned.

Putier immediately took a chef's position at another New York restaurant, where he worked for less than two weeks (still having not spoken with Brody), when one afternoon Brody called Putier at his new job. Wasting no words and making no explanations, Brody told Putier that he was to come back to work at the Rainbow Room and that Brody expected to see him in Brody's office that day at 3:00 PM. Fred Platzner had been fired.

That was thirty-five years ago, and Max Putier still believes that L'Étoile was the best French restaurant in New York and one of the best in the world. Every morsel of food served at L'Étoile was prepared entirely at L'Étoile. They butchered their own meat, prepared their own stocks, created their own pastries,and made daily twenty-six flavors of ice cream. There were no short cuts. Putier remembers the deadly stare Brody could and did deliver to those who did not admit their mistakes or who gave him shortshrift.

On a regular basis, Brody, Putier and the staff planned and revised the menu. Just after the luncheon crowd had left, Brody would often come into the kitchen of L'Étoile with a couple of guests to eat with the kitchen staff. They would sit at the refectory table on wooden benches, eating the same meal as the staff. Brody would not let Putier cook for them, because he wanted to experience what his customers experienced and nothing more.

The staff took pride in Brody's visits. They did not see him as an interloper or as a threat. His attention to their performance validated their commitment to his standards.

Brody made Putier executive chef of United Brody's entire

restaurant operations and expected Putier to dine at fine restaurants all over America and Europe. Brody would put thousands of dollars in cash in Putier's hands with the mandate to check out what the competition was doing, be it in Rome, Paris, or New York. Brody told Putier to tip twenty-percent.

L'Étoile was built on four levels. Glass balustrades along the floor landings were engraved with 500 famous French names such as Zola, Jouvet, Mistinguette, Le Coubusier, Descartes, Cendrars, and Bardot. The Brodys agreed that among them should appear none associated with war. If a body of Francophile New Yorkers, sophisticated enough to empathize with the engraved crystal roster of French culture, could be gathered, the display would serve a good marketing purpose. If not, the satisfaction in its creation would be like the stock bought way before its time: intellectual rather than financial.

If the celebration of the 500 was meant to evoke the greatness of French humane achievement, the architecture and design created by Alexander Girard was entirely a new creation, inspiring one reviewer to write "Paris wouldn't recognize it." Eschewing the red damask and gold leaf pomp of the grand tradition of French *cordon bleu* shrines such as Maxims, Lapérouse, Le Grand Véfour and Taillevent, Girard created spaces as clearcut and colorless as crystal. Two suspended stars revolved slowly, throwing out chips of light. Huge columns sheathed in metallic grays, soffits in matted black acoustic pan, and mirrored walls strove to transform structural elements into light. Abstract geometrical designs executed in various fabrics recalled the modernist school of geometrical painting. All was cool and clean and brilliant. One was made to feel he was in a showplace of the best of what had come to be called the *style moderne*, arousing visions of Vionnet, Chanel, the Dusenberg car, and Alexy Bradovich layouts.

125

The *à la carte* menu at L'Étoile listed just eight entrées and seven fish dishes against an assortment of sandwiches and *croustades* that included twenty-two items—a seeming imbalance that gave rise to the impression that L'Étoile was essentially "a snack bar." In Paris, Marlene Brody had come to admire the luncheon-style simple elegance of such restaurants as the Relais-Plaza. Instead of a heavy entrée from the *table d'hôte*, the Parisian will often lunch on something light from an *à la carte* menu. It was with these luncheon selections that L'Étoile meant to win New Yorkers to the lighter midday luncheon style of Paris. It was possible to order these lighter menu items even at dinner.

The *à la carte* luncheon menu included grillades, hearty salads, soufflées, including *soufflé L'Étoile* (a light cheese soufflé enclosing a poached egg), and *oeufs pochés Capucine* (poached eggs combined with creamed chicken and ham in a puff pastry with hollandaise sauce). There were exquisite croustades of cheese fondue made with Emmenthal, croques (*madam* and *monsieur*), *pissaladiére* (the Provence-style pizza) with anchovies, tomato, and black olives, and omelets.

But while luncheon was entirely *à la carte*, at dinner there was a *table d'hôte* right out of the great Escoffier-Brillat Savarin tradition. One might start with *galantine à la pistache* (molded boned chicken in aspic stuffed with ground veal and ham and flavored with pistachio nuts), *jambon persillé* (shredded cooked ham, combined with finely chopped fresh tarragon and parsley and a rich white wine flavored aspic, and molded into a loaf to be served in generous slices), *escargots à la bourguinonne*, clams Bercy (clams baked in a white wine sauce flavored with shallot), and *foies de volaille sur toast* (livers soaked in lightly salted water, then sautéed in a generous amount of sweet butter and garlic with a sprinkling of chopped parsley and a grating of nutmeg). Other *à la carte hors d'oeuvre*, included *oeuf en gelée au porto* (a perfectly poached egg, robed in *prosciutto* and set in a jelly of Port), and such hot dishes as *quiche de homard* (sautéed lobster, flamed with Cognac, swathed in an elegant custard, and baked in a delicate, thin pastry) and *saucisson en brioche* (a garlic sausage baked in a brioche). Alternate choices with the *table d'hôte* dinner included *consommé double*, vichyssoise madrilène and *bisques de crabe* (made with Alaskan King crab, rich fish broth, white wine, cream, and Cognac).

Among the entrées were *suprême de volaille fine champagne* (breast of chicken sautéed and the pan deglazed with Cognac and white wine to provide the basis for a cream sauce with morels), *homard Prince de Joinville* (sautéed lobster in a lobster sauce perfumed with Pernod and enriched with heavy cream), *ris de veau farci bouche du roi* (sweetbreads prepared with a stuffing of lobster mousse and a sauce of herb-seasoned cream flavored with Port) and *bar américaine* (sea bass stuffed with mousse of pike and served with two sauces, one of lobster and the other of white wine).

In addition to the *table d'hôte*, the *à la carte* selections included *poule au pot*, *boeuf bourguignonne* and medallions of veal with sliced, fresh mushrooms in cream.

Mimi Sheraton and Patrick Terrail had helped create the luxurious *table d'hôte* menu at L'Étoile, directed toward the sophisticated tastes of the international gourmet. Alongside it was the simpler and lighter style of the Parisian bistro lunch, which required from the customer for which it was unfamiliar, an accommodation to the tastes of management, an accommodation which ornery New Yorkers were notoriously unwilling to make. As it turned out, there was an inadequate base of such culinary sophistication to support such an expensive enterprise.

L'Étoile embraced too many competing elements: the grandness of its *table d'hôte* suggested a decor of plush and gold in the grand Parisian style, yet the abstract, airy modernism of Girard suggested the ambiance of a different world of lighter less formal dining, best exemplified by the *à la carte* luncheon menu. New Yorkers were not ready to enter a premier restaurant showcase in order to be served less than the rich *table d'hôte* banquets they expected when they were dining first-class. L'Étoile made the fatal mistake of being superior to the middle range of its potential customers. But over the course of a decade, it would receive high praise and develop a core of loyalists.

While L'Étoile was increasingly viewed as a triumph of French *haute cuisine* refinement, one of its major competitors for culinary fame remained the Four Seasons of Restaurant Associates, now under the presidency of Joe Baum, who was already engaged in his career-long practice of taking credit for Brody's successes.

Putier had firsthand experience of Baum's mytho-mania when Mimi Sheraton shared with Putier her great admiration for Baum, citing as evidence of his accomplishments Mama Leone's, the Forum of the Twelve Caesars, and the designs of the Four Seasons, La Fonda del Sol, and the Ground Floor. How Baum's preposterous claims came to be so widely believed is hard to comprehend. That Brody always refused to make it a public issue helped give Baum's assertions unhealthy life.

Putier adds an ironic footnote to the passing of L'Étoile in the late 1970s. After the closing of the restaurant, and now looking for a job, Max Putier answered a notice that the Rainbow Room, now managed and leased by Restaurant Associates, was looking for a chef. Putier was given an appointment and went to Restaurant Associates' company headquarters on Broadway, where Joe Baum, who apparently had forgotten that Putier and Brody had worked together for many years, interviewed him.

As might be expected, Baum was impressed by Putier's knowledge and found it interesting that Putier knew Brody. Baum described the days *when Brody had worked for him*, going on to take full credit for Brody's accomplishments. Putier could not hide his anger, and after giving Baum a piece of his mind, refused the job he had sought and just been offered.

Raffles and the
Sherry Netherland

Had the construction of the General Motors Building on the southeast corner of 59th Street and Fifth Avenue not been so long delayed there might never have been a Raffles, a name chosen by Cecil Beaton to recall the days of the gentleman Edwardian bandit of raffish England and the most famous of all the bars of the British Empire in Singapore. Brody, already the owner of L'Étoile and the Café Bar at the Sherry Netherland, acquired additional space in Serge Obolensky's old Carnaval Room, with plans to make it a luncheon club for the large invasion of expense account executives who were soon to work across the street.

A change in direction was called for, and Brody retained Earl Blackwell, of *Celebrity Register* fame, who had trotted out the "Beautiful People" for the Four Seasons and the Rainbow Room. The idea was to create an exclusive club for people of prestige, money, bloodlines, and style. As Brody was sadly to discover, at Raffles "exclusive," as Peter Benchley wrote in the *New York Times Magazine*, came to be applied in the "time-honored socioreligious sense of the word." Raffles opened in 1968, and within a year there were 1500 members of Raffles worldwide and a waiting list of about 1300.

Brody's choice of Beaton, the great British photographer and scenery and costume designer ("My Fair Lady") from the world of the theater, was a bold step. Having worked with brilliant designers before, men like William Pahlmann, Philip Johnson, and Alexander Girard, Brody intuited that Beaton's skill would be to deliver a mesmerizing evocation of a lost, elegant world still alive through nostalgia. This would be his gift to his customers, so used to luxury that only the unique could arouse their curiosity. Both Brody's inspiration and Beaton's magic made for what one reviewer called "instant heritage." It was just the thing to capture the "Beautiful People."

Interiors magazine described Beaton's Raffles as "a highly appreciative and witty summary of the fads and follies of the century, the interiors wend their way through *art nouveau*, Gibson girls, English Hunting scenes, theatrical posters, ending in a psychedelic trip in stained glass at the discotheque dance floor." The vaulted ceiling of the bar, which led down to the sunken dining room, was covered, as were the walls, in patterned green sackcloth. Beaton himself designed the carpet, also in green with splotches of red and black like ink spots and the formidable, elegant, brass chandelier was also a Beaton original, paying homage to the squirearchal elegance of the English Enlightenment.

The large dining room was divided into sections by plush velvet Scalamandré curtains on brass rails above the banquettes, making each table seem its own private space, while giving access to all the surroundings, like a private box at the opera. The disco floor at the far end of the dining room was Beaton's intrusion of the *de la mode* faddishness of the disco craze into his historical recreation of the past. Its psychedelic stained glass wall suggested the worship of pagan rather than divine powers. Its patterns were repeated intensely in the ceiling above the dance floor and then more mutedly elsewhere. The long corner lounge above the dining room was pure English-European gentlemen's club, the walls hung with hunting scenes, Matisses, Mondrians, and portraits of theatrical personalities, all in simple Hogarth frames, either in gold or black-and-gold.

Beaton's creation itself could have diverted attention from any crowd other than the narcissistic powerhouses who graced the roles of Raffles membership list. For them, nothing was more important than gaping at one another or, ideally, having others gape at them.

Blackwell said he "was looking for people representative of a certain standard that were also affable and gregarious." That phrase "a certain standard" was disingenuous cant standing for "rich WASPs" and the occasional European of such great wealth that his exotic birth could be overlooked. For that search, Blackwell chose fourteen men for a board of admissions and became their *eminence grise*.

An applicant had to be recommended in writing by three members of the admissions committee, which consisted of Charles Addams the cartoonist *but* of good family and a friend of the Kennedys; Harcourt Amory, Jr., a conservative Newport socialite; Andre Dubonnet, who founded "Corvilia," an exclusive skiing club in St. Moritz and whose family made the aperitif; Douglas Fairbanks and Henry Fonda, actors who looked like WASPs should; Francis L. Kellogg, in *the New York Social Register*; Frederick Melhado, "a young man who was very popular in Southampton"; David Metcalfe, a British investor; Bruno Pagliai the industrialist from Mexico who was married to Merle Oberon; George Plimpton, the socialite-sportsman with the good sense of humor; Count Teo Rossi, who like Andre Dubonnet had a family in the aperitif business and also belonged to a ski club in St. Moritz; Francis A. Shields, the son of the great tennis player of the same name, and many years later, the father of Brooke Shields, and Cornelius Vanderbilt Whitney, whose importance could be lost on no one.

The society columnist Eugenia Sheppard in an article for *Holiday* magazine reported the following Raffles constellation of big shots:

> Henry Ford was table-hopping. Around midnight he left the group that included his wife Christina, Merle Oberon and her husband, Bruno Pagliai, and moved over to Frank Sinatra's, where the guests around the big table were mostly men. Sinatra's party was rubbing elbows with Bob Evans, vice president of Paramount and his movie star wife, Ali McGraw, who were entertaining Bob's brother Charles and Henry Ford's daughter, Charlotte Niarchos. At a nearby table, Carol Channing was pulling a glass jar of minced buffalo meat, part of her rigorous diet, from a big handbag. She nibbled it delicately while hostess Mildred Custin and her guests, who included multimillionaire Charles Revson, ate steak.

Derek Hall-Caine, the English-born arbiter of taste in society matters, who ran Raffles, admitted that he was strict about letting only members in. Hall-Caine told the tale of informing some Secret Service men that President Johnson and one of his daughters would not be admitted unless they could latch onto a member. Hall-Caine claimed to have turned away Lord Snowdon, the son-in-law to his Queen. But even members of Raffles and the not-so-occasional non-member who gained entry by bribing the maitre d' at the door, according to Hall-Caine, were starstruck: "No matter who they are, they come here to see and be seen. Frank Sinatra likes to look at Henry Ford as much as Henry Ford likes to look at Sophia Loren. Mrs. Onassis likes to be told that over there, Bob Hope and Bing Crosby are sitting together."

Of the aspirants to "Beautiful Personhood," Hall-Caine observed, "They want to be told they're the Beautiful People. They want to see it in print. They feel they're important, and sitting next to a big name makes them believe it. When they see in the paper that so-and-so was at Raffles last night, they can say, 'I was there, too,' and they feel good. Obviously, there's a great deal of insecurity in all this."

When Brody and Blackwell first decided on a membership board, Brody agreed that even if he wanted to get his brother in, he wouldn't do so without going through the board. Sometime later, Brody, true to his word, proposed for membership his good friend, Cy Lewis, the head of Bear Sterns. There was a lot of negative shaking of heads, which Brody interpreted as WASP disapproval of aggressive Jewish money. He told them there was no way on earth that Cy Lewis was not getting into Raffles. He was admitted. The board did not fancy Jews as members of Raffles, although there were a few, including John Revson, the son of the multimillionaire cosmetic executive who was married to Brody's daughter, Ricki. Brody recalls unexpectedly running into Philip Johnson at the bar of Raffles. Johnson was delighted to see Brody, but very surprised. The first thing Johnson said was "What are you doing here?" Brody told him. He never saw Johnson in the club again. For Johnson, who had ardently supported Adolf Hitler, Raffles had become unattractive.

More than forty years later, Brody recalling the heyday of Raffles felt that from the moment of that membership committee decision, Raffles began to unwind, perhaps, because the elitist WASP socialites at its center, felt it had lost some of its exclusiveness. Brody, who had come to believe that a restaurant was great "only so long as the owner had his heart in it," had, perhaps, at that moment, withdrawn his.

The food service at Raffles was notoriously slow because

Raffles customers were served from the same kitchen that served the bar upstairs and L'Étoile around the corner. But not one member resigned over the food service. In the first year, however forty-four members were not invited back for transgressions such as non-payment and misbehavior. A case in point being two ladies who were guests of a member, who rose from their dining banquette, walked arm in arm to the dance floor, and danced with one another. One wonders what would have happened to the membership rolls if, in addition to uni-sex dancing, alcoholism and cocaine addiction were reasons for dismissal.

It would take, however, much more than slow food service to dampen the hectic gaiety of Raffle's "Beautiful People"—something like a recession.

When Brody had taken control of the restaurant operations of the Sherry Netherland, his staff would be servicing not only the Café Bar, and Raffles, but also room service for hotel guests and owners of cooperative apartments within the hotel. Brody did not foresee the endemic difficulties which would hound the room service operation, and, in turn, adversely affect his other Sherry Netherland enterprises. Not only did room service operate 24-hour hours, but also the entire menu was available to room service guests of the Sherry Netherland no matter what the hour, and nothing could be scrimped in terms of luxurious presentation. The burden on the chefs to fulfill the requests of one room service individual while preparing entirely different offerings for the regular luncheon and dinner crowds was onerous. The necessity for extra staff, often on idle stand-by was expensive. The ability to predict demand was hampered by the irregularity of room service ordering patterns. Even if L'Étoile, the Café Bar, and Raffles were not already operating out of shared resources, room service would have been tactically and financially annoying.

When the recession hit, it became disastrous, and for a time, Brody thought that bankruptcy was inevitable. As the financial burden on Brody increased and Brody's capacity to borrow through the hard times was strained beyond limit, a white knight appeared from out of the blue: Gerard Oestreicher, a successful real estate developer who Brody admired but with whom he had never had a close friendship or business dealings. When Brody told Oestreicher about his financial problems at the Sherry Netherland, Oestreicher volunteered to co-sign Brody's loan with the banks, no further questions asked. That last minute reprieve saved the day, although it could not eliminate the pain.

The 1950s and 1960s had been the most prosperous years in America's and the world's history. Starved by the Depression and the economies of the World War II, the American consumer, urged on by Madison Avenue and its powerful new ally television, started spending with a vengeance. The cost of spending to counter the threat of Russian communism further drove production and wages upwards. And as consumer spending increased and the distinction between the necessities and luxuries blurred, it must have seemed to some that the nation's output was limitless—as was its supply of restaurant customers.

The cost of the war in Vietnam and the programs of the Great Society began to put strains on the system. Prices, responding to shortages, began to rise in the late 1960s and the Arab oil embargo of 1973 sent them rocketing. American inflation made it easier for Japan and Germany to compete in the American marketplace, especially in the automotive business. The halls of the General Motors Building, across 59th Street from the Sherry Netherland were filled with fear, if not with panic. Of course, the stock market nose-dived, and Wall Street brokers and Wall Street investors alike were eating their hearts out rather than eating out in Brody's restaurants. These events brought United

Brody to the brink of bankruptcy.

Only Gallagher's would weather the storm, but in the midst of the storm, Brody would be given the opportunity to begin another restaurant venture which would match the enormous success of Gallagher's.

The Grand Central
Oyster Bar

By 1972, things had gotten so bad that an eviction notice had been placed on the door of the Brody's apartment at 200 Central Park South. Along with dozens of other fine dining restaurants, Brody's holdings were being gutted by the severe recession of the early 1970s. Many owners hounded by creditors, declared bankruptcy or stopped answering telephone calls. Brody reacted differently.

Brody had left a standing order to his managers that he was to be summoned personally to answer telephone calls from any creditor. This applied not only during working hours. Brody told Marlene that he was always available to speak to anyone to whom he owed money. Not only was Brody confident that he would survive the crisis, but he was in a fighting mood, anxious to see what creative opportunities the economic shake up would present to him. Brody had been strong even before he had found a soul mate in his wife, Marlene, but now that their life together brought them so much joy, he was more resilient than ever.

In 1974, apart from Gallagher's, United Brody Corp. was on the ropes. But one would never have guessed it from Brody's demeanor. So it was with full expectation that he was placing his proposal before a vital restaurant executive that Stan Lewis, the head of real estate for the Metropolitan Transit Authority, over a lunch at Gallagher's, suggested that Brody take over the premises and the business of the once proud, but now derelict, Grand Central Oyster Bar. Brody thought instantly that he might have another Gallagher's on his hands. The MTA advanced Brody seventy-five thousand dollars for renovation and Brody spent about twice that in order to open the doors once again.

The Oyster Bar had first opened its doors in 1913 on the lower level of Grand Central Terminal. Woodrow Wilson was President, the United States was on the threshold of World War I, and Prohibition was six years away. New York City was slowly emerging as a literary and artistic center and little "salons" that attracted writers and artists and dilettantes were starting to spring up in Greenwich Village and in other parts of the city. The resplendent new Grand Central Terminal opened its doors that year too, on the site of what formerly had been the old and run-down train depot. People flocked to see the new terminal that was, then as now, considered an engineering marvel.

For almost 60 years the old Oyster Bar remained a landmark. But despite its fame, Brody knew that the long-lived acceptance of the restaurant was based more on its location at the hub of America's long-haul passenger train system than on its food and service. With the decline of the long-haul passenger train system came the decline of the restaurant. It had no position among New York restaurants, and while thousands of commuters passed by everyday, very few went inside to eat.

In 1974, when Brody was approached by the New York Metropolitan Transit Authority to take it over, the old restaurant had been bankrupt and empty for two years, having become in its last days not much more than a sad, old coffee shop. Brody inspected what remained of its former grandness. The elegant marble columns in the restaurant today were then painted aquamarine over wallpaper. The wall covering was yellow Cello-tex. The furniture was upholstered yellow, in unsettling contrast with the red tablecloths. The famous Guastavino tiles were black with grime.

Despite the obvious drawbacks and failures of the old restaurant, Brody thought that if he could develop a strong merchandising concept, the 440-seat space had real potential. But it would be up to Brody to invent a new restaurant—from menu to decor—which would *make* the Oyster Bar a destination restaurant just as certainly as Gallagher's was one.

The old Oyster Bar, while its name suggested seafood, was not, in fact, a seafood restaurant. Its oyster stew had become famous, but the rest of the menu could best be described as "continental." The job of invention would start from scratch— but seafood it would be.

To prepare for making this decision, Brody and Marlene toured the best-known seafood restaurants in Manhattan, Brooklyn, New Jersey, and the rest of the metropolitan area; they were invariably full even when the cuisine was ordinary. In 1974, Brody entered into a lease with the MTA and embarked upon reinventing the Grand Central Oyster Bar & Restaurant.

It was essential that the Oyster Bar develop a network of the best suppliers. In Maine, Brody and Marlene searched for lobster, in Gloucester, Massachusetts, for the best fish from the Grand Banks, in Virginia, for oysters and crabs from the Chesapeake Bay. Brody got invaluable advice from A.J. McClane, the author of authoritative *The Encyclopedia of Fish*. McClane identified species of fish such as *loup* (wolfish), which were not served in American restaurants, but which were known to European gourmets. To this day, the Grand Central Oyster Bar & Restaurant continues to cultivate and reach out to a great number of international suppliers, ranging from large corporations to individual fishermen, with whom over the years it has developed a privileged relationship. It also stays in contact with individual small boat skippers who will call the Oyster Bar when they have hoodked into a big halibut.

Once Brody was confident that he had ample access to the best, fresh seafood, the next step was to test their menu in their own kitchens. So Brody and his staff spent a tremendous amount of time deciding not only what to have on the menu but on methods of preparation. Even an apparently basic technique like broiling was subject to the closest scrutiny. But whatever was prepared, Brody insisted that the hallmark of the Oyster Bar be the best, fresh fish available, presented in a bright, clean, manner.

Because the Oyster Bar aspired to be a great American seafood restaurant, Brody set out to develop a superb American white wine list. As carefully as he had sought out seafood suppliers, his manager, Mario Staub, exhaustively selected their wine wholesalers and vintners, who, to this day, name the white wine cellars of the Grand Central Oyster Bar among the best in the country. The Oyster Bar won the Brotherhood of the Knights of the Vine "Gold Vine Award" in 1978 and 1979, "The Wine Spectator" honored the Oyster Bar with its Award of Excellence in 1996, and in 1999, the Oyster Bar won the James Beard Award.

The Oyster Bar constantly looks for unusual items, such as summer oysters now available, in this age of refrigerated air transport, from the Southern Hemisphere. Brody's stewards search out products from the ever-increasing stocks made available through aquaculture. They test cook new sauces to accommodate customers' desire for less butter and cream. Every day they monitor the computer records of what is popular with their customers and what is not.

Brody is proud of the Oyster Bar; for him, the proof of its ability to give the customer what he wants is in its longevity. Brody says, "In this marketplace a restaurant opens and gets a lot of play, but what happens a year later? What happens 25 years later? Brody had learned painfully how quickly fame can vanish. "To have flourished for these 25 years, that is success."

In 1975, Brody decided not renew his lease at the Rainbow Room. In short order, all his restaurant holdings and management contracts with the exception of Gallagher's and the Grand Central Oyster Bar, would be history. The income from the two restaurants was considerable and it was, by the standards of the restaurant business, safe. While dreams of a multi-restaurant, international corporation had flickered to life and then flickered out, new dreams filled the Brodys' hearts and minds.

Jerry Brody was about to become a gentleman farmer.

Winter Dreams

In addition to the aggravations of business, Grace, who married Bob Forrest, Danny Kaye's brother-in-law, was making contact with the children as difficult as the rules of their separation agreement would allow. During one visitation period, Brody wanted to take his son Scott to Monaco to coincide with the festival Princess Grace was planning and which Gallagher's would cater. Grace denied Scott permission to leave the country. Brody and Marlene substituted a yacht cruise for Scott, which would culminate in a vacation on Nantucket. On the day Scott was supposed to be delivered back to his mother, all flights from Nantucket were canceled because of fog. Brody asked Scott to call his mother with the news. Scott returned from the phone and reported that Grace demanded that Scott not miss the deadline set out in the visitation agreement no matter what the weather. If he did, there would be hell to pay.

Brody, Marlene, and Scott set out for the mainland in a chartered boat, in weather which kept even experienced captains in harbor. With Brody doing the navigating, they miraculously brushed up against the buoy to their harbor of destination, and Scott was returned to the care of his mother on time.

Brody's daughter Ricki, a wildly popular girl in school and now a real beauty, was being courted by John Revson, the son of the multimillionaire cosmetics executive, who was very much of the fast social set. Raffishly good-looking and footloose, Revson, in the opinion of both Grace and Brody (in one of the few times they agreed on a course of action for the children) was idle and insubstantial. They both advised against the marriage, which nonetheless took place and which was a grand affair made so by Brody's characteristic genius as a party giver.

During subsequent visits with Ricki, Marlene and Brody saw that life had become a burden for her. With their aid and advice, Ricki sought help, both psychological and medical, but her distress went unabated. In 1972 Ricki died. Brody was devastated. Clearly 1972 was a time when both personal and business problems challenged Marlene and Brody with a full dose of the harshness that life inevitably administers.

The cash flow problems attendant upon the disappointing performances of L'Étoile, Raffles, and the Sherry Netherland enterprises were aggravating. Creditors called at all hours of the day and night and Brody never avoided them. And while he bore up under the slings and arrows with strength and stoicism, Marlene knew that he desperately needed a rest. She set out to find them a place in the country.

The Brodys had rented a summerhouse on the dunes in ultra-fashionable East Hampton during the summers of 1968, 1969 and 1970. A summer in the Hamptons is for those who keep up with the social whirl, hardly a bucolic interlude, but the Brodys succeeded in keeping a low profile. It was only after Ricki divorced that the Brodys joined the social set and it is not surprising that they did not like it at all. In any case, even if they had looked forward to the Vanity Fair of the Hamptons, they could no longer afford the expense. Besides, summer was too far off and Marlene was determined to find them a getaway somewhere and sooner rather than later.

That winter, after combing the pages of the *New York Times* real estate section, Marlene found a rental offering for a two-bedroom cottage on sixty secluded acres in Columbia County New York, which in those days prior to its revival and gentrification was remote, unfashionable, and rural. The rent was two hundred dollars a month. When Marlene told Brody about the house, Brody said that $200 was too much money and besides, at that price the place was probably a dump. Undeterred, Marlene, during a stroll in Central Park, told her friend Doreen Flemington about the house. Doreen, married to Roger Flemington, recently sent from London to New York to establish a branch of National Westminster Bank, found the notion of a place in the country attractive. Roger, too, had been working himself too hard.

The ladies made a one day round trip to Columbia County. They both loved the cottage and Marlene convinced Brody to inspect it. His only condition was that the owner, Addie Wallin, let them spend the night. When that proved to be no obstacle, Marlene, Brody, Doreen and Roger visited the cottage together. There was universal approval. Marlene and Brody had two English setters, Heathcliffe and Digby. They would have to be welcome, Brody insisted, hoping to initiate some obstacle. But the dogs were welcome. Brody and Flemington signed the deal.

For the next two years, the Brodys spent many of their winter weekends at the cottage. They both loved the house and the countryside. There was time for long walks on dirt paths and through the winter forests. In a way it was appropriate that this period of healing and preparation for new growth was the winter dormancy that makes the energies of new growth possible.

The surrounding countryside was dotted with apple farms

and dairies. The Hudson River was five miles to the west and beyond that the beautiful hills and mountains of the Catskills. The Brodys traveled all over Columbia County, getting a feel for it, and developing an easy peace within its rural confines that would make their decision to found Gallagher's Stud the outgrowth of comfortable familiarity.

In that first year, Marlene remembers best that Jerry got lots of sleep and, with his revitalization coincidentally, came a slow, but steady recovery of business fortunes. Gallagher's performed well and so did the Rainbow Room. When another and larger house down the road from the cottage became available for summer rental, the Brodys were prepared to take it. However, it was still their plan to winter at the "Winter Palace," as the cottage was now known.

The new pink house (the "Summer Palace") was part of a working farm owned by the Johnson family. The rent by Hampton standards was tiny: $700 per month. The caretaker of the house loved animals, and goats, sheep, dogs, and horses meandered about the grounds. The Brodys loved their first summer at the "Summer Palace" and were prepared to rent it for yet another year. That winter they were especially pleased when Brody's daughter, Kathy phoned from California to say that she and her husband Michael would like to spend at least a month with them and that she wanted to bring her children, Jason and Marisa.

Marlene and Brody were eager for the visit, but he was troubled that in the last year the caretaker had lost his job to the recession and had sold the animals for cash. Brody was not about to have his grandchildren visit a farm with no animals on it. Something had to be done. The place could do with an animal or two.

Brody figured that with so many dairy and cattle farms in the neighborhood, it ought to be relatively easy to acquire an attractive animal that would amuse Kathy's children. Jack Solomon, the previous owner of Gallagher's Steak House had been a breeder of Angus cattle, and pictures of some of Solomon's proudest Angus champions still hung in the restaurant. Perhaps that was the subliminal prompt when Brody drove with Marlene to an Angus farm in their neighborhood.

The Sir William farm was owned by Leon Rubin, who had made his fortune by importing Krakus-Atalantis Polish hams. Rubin had used part of his fortune to gain entry not only into the rarefied world of Angus breeding but also into the world of Arabian thoroughbreds, the proud breed which had been the ornament of the royal houses of Poland for centuries.

Brody was unaware of Rubin's *bona fides* when he approached Ira Boggs, the farm manager of Sir William, and asked if he might buy an animal. What Brody did not then know was that the farm he and Marlene had stumbled upon was the foremost Angus breeding farm in the world. It is as if Brody had walked in off the Rue de Rivoli and asked the curator of the Louvre if he had some spare paintings for sale.

The farm manager said that the farm's Angus cattle were about to be put up for sale at a show the coming weekend in Phelps. Brody asked if he could buy something immediately and the manager said that he would put together a group of cattle for Brody to look at.

Columbia County and Dutchess County just to the south were in the forefront of Angus breeding. They had had national champions for many years and before that, New York had been an Angus breeding capital. But New York State seemed to take no pride in its pre-eminence.

If the Brodys wanted to attend next week's Angus auction, Ira Boggs told them, the Sir William Farm would be glad to helicopter them to Phelps. Brody was impressed. Brody, now sensing the disparity between what he knew about Angus and what he knew he had better know if he were to be treated fairly, decided to do some research.

Brody took home the Sir William catalogue and studied it in preparation for next week's auction. When the day of the auction arrived, the weather was so windy that the helicopter was grounded. But Brody would not be deterred, and he, Marlene, and the two dogs, traveled to Phelps, New York in order to bid on at least one Angus.

The first animal, which was led out for auction, was Mignonne. Brody bought her for $5,000, an enormous sum. He was so inexperienced in the ways of cattle auctions that he feels to this day that he accidentally bid against himself, driving up the price. Subsequently, the Brodys bought three or four other Angus cows, but this time for only hundreds of dollars, emphasizing the relative enormity of the $5,000 he had paid for Mignonne.

The Brodys were now Angus owners, but they did not have a farm. They had arranged to winter the cattle at Leon Rubin's Sir William Farm. The Brodys spent their winter weekends at the Winter Palace and prepared to move into the pink Summer Palace on Memorial Day weekend. Arrangements were made for Mignonne and her lesser Brody Angus colleagues to be moved to the Summer Palace, but not before the staff of Sir William Farm repaired the fencing.

No sooner were Mignonne and company ensconced at the Summer Palace than Mignonne gave birth to a bull calf, which the experts at the Sir William Farm said was the most beautiful Angus bull calf the world had ever seen.

Whatever the merits of that judgment, certainly Kathy's children shared that opinion, and they spent a great summer with the Brodys adoring their Angus pets. Jason in fact turned out to be quite a hero. Jason's crying that the bull calf had escaped the corral awakened Kathy and her husband Michael. At first they thought he was having a bad dream. But Mignonne was wailing in distress. Robbie, her beautiful bull calf, was wailing, also. After some difficulty Mignonne and Robbie were reunited with no damage done to either.

That winter Brody immersed himself in the study of Angus breeding. As he had in the restaurant business, it was only when he had first-hand knowledge of his subject that he felt confident enough to make a full commitment. But full commitments were a characteristic of Brody's business successes, and, by the next spring even Angus breeding experts were amazed by his knowledge.

That same winter, Leon Rubin had gone on safari to Africa. While flying in a his private plane he had ventured too high and had suffered a serious dose of anoxia. Now convalescing back at his Sir William Farm, the bedridden Rubin had made up his mind to sell his Angus herd.

While the Brodys were paying the convalescent a visit, Rubin offered to sell his entire herd to Brody. Rubin knew of Brody's reputation in the restaurant business, not only in masterminding rapid expansion but also in creating startling and uniquely luxurious venues with no precedent in New York City. Rubin also knew that Brody's daring was based on an unshakeable reliance on exhaustive research. Anyone who would successfully carry on the legacy of Sir William Farm would need just such a set of characteristics.

There are 300,000 registered Angus in the United States but only about 300 compete at the championship level. By now Brody knew these daunting statistics. Rubin might be offering Brody a unique opportunity but the risk would still be enormous.

From his bed, Rubin said, "Jerry, you've got to buy my herd."

"Leon," said Brody, "Just because I'm wearing sneakers doesn't mean that I am a rich eccentric! But, if you want to show us your operating statements, we might be able to work something out."

During the long period while Rubin was gathering (or inventing) his operating statements, Brody had long conversations with Rubin's farm manager, Ira Boggs. Brody suggested that Boggs himself become part of a group that would buy the Rubin interest. Boggs declined to become part of such a group with Brody and he found buyers for the herd. However, he also decided that Brody's interests in the Angus world deserved to be encouraged. He agreed to notify Brody when he saw cattle that he thought Brody should buy.

Brody and Marlene traveled with Boggs to some of the more important cattle shows and at the suggestions of Boggs would buy one or two more Angus. Even in later years, when their thoroughbred racing horses competed at the highest international levels, would the Brodys be as excited as they were at these Angus shows and competitions

The Angus owner, his animal awaiting judgment against other prize competitors, waits in the packed bleachers, which grow ever more silent as the owners of the dwindling select await the final decision. When the winner is chosen, the bleachers explode in a roar of approbation. When the championship silverware is handed over to the winning owner, the thrill of victory is intense: the victor becomes part of a world of remarkable Americans about whom not much is known outside of the world of Angus people themselves.

Marlene, a European, noted that Angus people were often the descendants of American pioneering families who had lived on the land for generations and for whom the land had become a deep-down attachment, stronger than business—a way of life— almost a religion.

But they were also often an unexpected hybrid of social and economic privilege yoked to rough-hewn self-reliance. They had a directness and a personal responsibility to day-to-day operations and to the people who worked for them, which was rare to find at the top echelons of business and finance.

And Angus people were, almost without exception, risk takers—people who tied up millions of dollars in huge farms—all on the uncertain promise of succeeding in a financially doubtful enterprise. These were people with whom Brody felt at ease and with whom he was delighted to find common cause.

Boggs's new investment group, the group that bought the Rubin herd, took the herd to that January's Western National Stock Show in Denver, the top agricultural show in the nation. The Brodys accompanied Boggs and the new Angus group. The Rubin herd featured the champion bull, Excursion, on whom the new group were pinning their hopes to verify the wisdom of their new purchase by winning the first time out under his new colors. However, Excursion came in second; spirits in the Boggs camp were low.

Nonetheless, Boggs beckoned Marlene and Brody over to the show string of Kansas State University, which had had the Angus heifer calf state champion by Great Northern. Boggs, who had right of first refusal on the heifer calf because he had supplied the semen that had created her, waived his right, and Brody bought the calf then called Miss Northern K 195, for $5,000.
Under the purchase agreement Kansas State would keep Miss Northern K 195 and bring her back to the show circuit the next season. After the next Denver show, Ken Conroy, the manager of the Kansas State Angus program, would return her to the Brodys.

Kansas had never had a star like Miss Northern K 195 before and its desire to keep her at Kansas State is analogous to a top ten basketball university's desire to keep a media star coach. Years later, the fame of Manhattan Gal (née Miss Northern K195) is still a potent recruiting tool, bringing student cattlemen to Kansas State in the hopes of replicating that success.

A couple of weeks after the purchase of Miss Northern K 195, Brody called Kansas State University and said it had occurred to him that the Brodys lived in Manhattan, New York and that Kansas State was in Manhattan, Kansas. How would Kansas State feel about changing Miss Northern K 195's name to Manhattan Gal ("Gal" as in Gallagher's). There were no objections.

The following year, Kansas State took Manhattan Gal out on the show circuit. The first big championship was the Futurity in Louisville, Kentucky. The Brodys attended the show and, upon their arrival, various people told them that Manhattan Gal was going to win. They were right. Manhattan Gal became the Champion heifer. On their way to the judges' stan, Marlene was intercepted by some cattle enthusiast who asked, "So, how many do have in your show string?" Marlene replied, "One."

Apart from his excitement and pride at such a victory, Brody felt almost embarrassed. So many of the people there had put their lives into breeding; the Brodys had won with their first Angus and in their first year.

At the Futurity in Louisville, a champion bull was also selected, and then the champion bull and the champion heifer were matched off, and a Supreme Champion chosen. Manhattan Gal became the third heifer in thirty years to become Supreme Champion, a feat roughly equal to a filly's winning the Kentucky Derby and the rest of the Triple Crown.

While Manhattan Gal was establishing her superiority in the ranks of the heifers, Patriot was doing the same among the Angus bulls. In January 1978, Patriot was judged Grand Champion bull at the Western National Stock Show in Denver.

Brody and Marlene had witnessed Patriot's triumph in Denver, and were told that the *New York Times* would run a story in the next day's morning edition. After returning to New York that evening, Brody awoke the next morning in his Central Park South apartment and eagerly raced through the various sections of the *New York Times*, angry and disappointed to find no mention of Patriot.

Routinely, Brody began his restaurant rounds with a 7:30 AM visit to the Oyster Bar. He complained to the staff that no word of Patriot had appeared in the *New York Times*, and slammed the paper down on a counter. Brody's manager was dumbfounded. He took Brody's copy of the *Times* and pointed to the first page, the only place Brody had neglected to look.

Having given up the summer lease on the pink Summer Palace, and with Boggs now unwilling to winter Brodys' small herd for a second season, the Brodys' herd was with another Columbia County farmer, Richard White. It was clear that by the next year the Brodys would have to buy a farm if Manhattan Gal was to have a place to rest her royal body. The Brodys purchased a farm in Ghent, New York. Manhattan Gal and the rest of the Angus herd now had a home. To help them build the farm and the herd the Brodys hired a young man who had been at Sir William Farm, Kevin O'Brien.

Gallagher's Stud

The opportunity arose to buy one hundred acres of farm land and lease another ninety in Ghent, New York, just minutes from the Winter and Summer Palaces. The Brodys, who had searched extensively, finally found a property which had gone on the market upon the retirement of the elderly farm owner. Brody and Marlene liked what they saw, but their two English setters, Heathcliffe and Digby, acted as if they had found heaven. Marlene still believes that the decision to buy was made by the dogs. Negotiations went smoothly, and for $132,000, Brody bought the first one hundred acres of what would eventually grow into the six hundred fifty acres of the present Gallagher's Stud.

The farmland in this part of Columbia County rises gradually from the plain of the Hudson River to the west into gentle rolling hills and meadows. Where the land has not been cleared for farming, tall deciduous oak, maple, birch and willow grow in forest density, so that the autumnal leaf display is as beautiful as anywhere else in the Northeast. Fresh water rivulets meander through weed-choked bottomland, all draining toward the Hudson. It is good country for grazing, once the cattle have added enough fertilizer to the soil to encourage the grass. The rolling

Ricki and her brother Scott, who is now general manager of radio station WXRV in Boston, and the father of three.

Cathy with Ricki, the bride of John Revson.

Rose and Jac Brody at their 50th wedding anniversary gala, hosted by their son.

Brody and daughter, Kathy, Jackson, Wyoming, 1996.

Adorable Micol with her son
by Storm Cat, Adcat. (Marlene Brody photo)

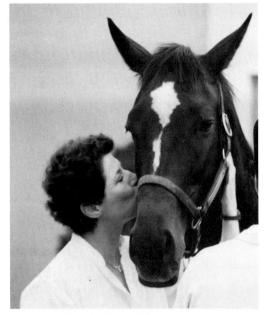

Manhattan Gal, the Brodys' first racing filly,
like her Angus namesake, turned out to be
a winner. Marlene shows her appreciation.

The Brodys chart every imaginable vital fact concerning their horses, from racing performance to genetics, to racing schedules, to jockeys, to matings, etc.

Brody with Guy Harwood at Harwood's private training center, Pulborough, England. Allez Milord was in training to Harwood during his triumphal campaign of 1985.

Allez Milord winning the $250,000 Grade 1 Oak Tree Invitational under a great ride by Chris McCarron.

Brody and Marlene celebrate their 25th
wedding anniversary at the Grand Central
Oyster Bar, May 8, 1989.

The Brodys with painter Pierre Alechinsky in front
of the Palais Royal in Paris. Alechinsky was given
a one-man show at Le Jeu de Paume in Paris, to
which the Brodys loaned masterpieces from their
own collection.

Marlene with the poet and
novelist Michael Onjaatje,
during a 1995 cruise aboard
Bonheur 2 from Belize to
Cancun. (Marga Clark photo)

When Brody took over the Grand Central Oyster Bar in 1974, it had been bankrupt and derelict. Now in its 26th year under Brody, having survived the fire of 1998, it re-opened in the refurbished Grand Central Station, and is doing enormous business, almost triple the hefty norms of the past.

Captain Blair Albert stands next to Jim Gilbert, editor of *Showboat Magazine*.

The Brodys aboard Bonheur 2 voted by *Showboats Magazine*, "the best new charter yacht in the world." Bonheur 2 was 130 feet long and 26' 9" in the beam. It had five guest cabins, which slept 10, and had a crew of seven. It had a maximum speed of 18 knots. Its appointments, its galley, and its staff, made it at least as beautiful and comfortable as the most splendid of Brody's restaurants and was located in a much more beautiful neighborhood.

Back at the farm, Brody, pet poodle Rocky and pet cat Hollywood taking care of business.

(John Lefebre photo)

hills "muscle up" the cattle as they graze their way through the fields. The county is famous for its apple groves and the river, which runs its entire length, would still be one of the great suppliers of striped bass if the Hudson had not been polluted by PCBs dumped many years ago from the General Electric plant upstream in Schenectady.

The Dutch were the first European settlers of the lands along the river and their place names are present in its cities and villages: Rhinebeck, Hudson, Kinderhook, and Ghent. When the English displaced the Dutch, they added their own place names: Albany, Nassau, Kingston, Livingston, and Saratoga. Columbia County is part of the landscape celebrated by the Hudson River School painters, most famous among them Thomas Cole, Albert Bierstadt, and Frederick Edwin Church.

The summers are muggy. Along the river, in cities such as Hudson, it is steamy, and on many summer days, one wishes that the southwest winds of summer were not so often blocked by the Catskills, which run north to south astride the Hudson. Winters are a different matter, when the Arctic winds from the North blast down the Hudson Valley. It is on those infrequent, crisp days of summer that one wishes there could be a Columbia County tradeoff between the north wind of winter and the southwest wind of summer.

Nineteen-year-old Phil Trowbridge knew all about those winds. He had been brought up on a cattle farm outside Buffalo but in his college years, had spent summers working on the Sir William Farm. Trowbridge knew how to build, to repair, to carry and to work hard. He was big and strong and young. He was also smart, and was prepared to put to good use what he had learned at agricultural college. But he had seen almost nothing of the world beyond rural New York State. He was definitely small-town; he had never been on a plane or owned a credit card. The two things he was confident about were his knowledge of cattle and his knowledge of how to build and fix anything on a farm.

Brody had first heard Trowbridge's name from Kevin O'Brien, the assistant farm manager of Sir William. In the winter of 1976, Brody asked O'Brien to become the manager of Brody's new farm and O' Brien accepted. With Manhattan Gal about to arrive in the spring of 1977, O'Brien needed a herdsman and general righthand man to help get the new farm in working order. O'Brien called Trowbridge who agreed to an interview with Brody.

Marlene and Brody met Trowbridge at a diner in nearby Hillsdale. He was amazed by how much the Brodys knew about cattle. Trowbridge knew that the Brodys were very new to the business, but the questions they asked about agriculture and about breeding made him think that he was dealing with people with the kind of long-term ambitions he shared. Instead of the usual job interview queries about where he went to school and what were his strongest interests, Brody asked him a question that in and of itself convinced Trowbridge to take the job: To whom he should breed Manhattan Gal? Trowbridge felt that Brody was inviting Trowbridge to contribute to an essential decision. It made him feel that Brody took him seriously.

When Trowbridge agreed to a salary of five hundred dollars per month, Brody wrote out a contract on a piece of scratch paper. That made Trowbridge a little uncomfortable; all his deals before then had been sealed by a handshake.

At the time that Phil Trowbridge agreed to work for the Brodys, they had just bought the farm. Trowbridge remembers that there was nothing on it—no livestock, no useable barns, no fencing. The residence was in shambles, unfit for habitation. Brody, O' Brien and he would have the opportunity to plan and build Gallagher's Stud from the ground up.

The work that first winter and spring was enormous;

Trowbridge remembers that he was glad he was only twenty years old. Kevin O'Brien and Brody talked all the time about how they were going to lay the farm out, with the premium on efficiency, which to Brody was an essential ingredient in any commercial design. Trowbridge was allowed his say.

Only one barn would be erected that first year, but O'Brien and Trowbridge had this kind of work so much in their blood, that the design had become intuitive. The same was true of the fences. Both men knew that the cattle had to be protected from the wind; it was second nature to them to fence in the corrals to maximize the well being of the herd. Every decision was discussed with Brody.

In 1976, the minimum essential fencing and one barn was completed. 1977 started grandly with the completion of Manhattan Gal's Triple Crown at Denver. Manhattan Gal would be a tough act to follow.

On March 26th, 1977, Phil Trowbridge got married. The wedding was held three hundred miles away in Rochester. The Brodys hired a private plane in order to attend the wedding. For Phil Trowbridge that kind of attention made a lasting impression. He felt part of the family. It drew him even closer to the farm.

Only two days later, on March 28th, Trowbridge and his bride were driving back to Ghent. Trowbridge wanted to be back at work as soon as possible. On their way past Syracuse, at 6:00 AM, they stopped off to visit the farm of Princeton alumnus, Sayre McCleod. As Trowbridge got out of his car, he saw a bull calf that stopped him in his tracks.

Trowbridge was stunned by the perfection of that calf and raced back to Gallagher's Stud to share his enthusiasm with Kevin O'Brien. When a week went by without O'Brien's taking any action, Trowbridge and O'Brien got into a "discussion" about the calf, which was overheard by Brody. Brody, trusting that Trowbridge's excitement was likely to be based on solid evidence, immediately informed O'Brien that both of them would visit the Sayre farm immediately.

O'Brien's initial skepticism disappeared at the sight of the bull calf. But Mark Richardson, the farm manager, knew the value of what he had and drove the price up to $50,000 and that for only a half share. The bull calf's name was Patriot, and Brody bought him on the spot.

Brody's apparently impetuous purchase of Patriot, who would become one of America's most celebrated prize bulls, was characteristic of the way Brody operated. The large price and the quick decision took courage, but Brody had made the considered judgment that Trowbridge was to be trusted and that his immense excitement over Patriot was not to be ignored. Trowbridge and O'Brien's praise of the animal meshed with what Brody had learned about Angus and he was not assailed by second thoughts.

Patriot's rare beauty caused a buzz in the Angus industry even before the Futurity in Louisville, where the year's best bulls would be showcased. Kevin O'Brien accompanied Patriot to the Futurity. Back at Gallagher's Stud, the Brodys awaited news that Patriot was as good as everyone thought. But when the call from O'Brien came in to the farm, the news was disastrous. Mark Richardson had not tattooed Patriot properly and Patriot, therefore, was ineligible to compete.

The next morning at 9:00 am, Brody chartered a private plane to Louisville, but not before commanding Trowbridge to give him Patriot's tattoo pliers with the number "434H." If Brody had to tattoo Patriot himself, that was what he was going to do. Brody arrived in Louisville and did everything short of violence to get the officials of the Futurity to cut him some slack. But his efforts were futile; Brody was both angry and frustrated. But now he was more determined than ever to let no more time go by before Patriot's excellence was confirmed in the show ring.

The very next week was the Illinois State Fair, but the entry deadline had passed. Brody pulled strings. By now Brody's name was known around the Angus business, and the *cognoscenti* wanted him as an ally. Brody prevailed on the Weaver family, the most influential Angus breeders in Illinois, to use their influence to get Patriot in as a late entry, which they did. In the finals, Patriot came up against Empire Maverick, who had won the Futurity in Louisville. Patriot vanquished Empire Maverick and then went on to win all the important competitions in which he was involved. In January of the following year, Patriot culminated his triumphant progress at Denver, just as Manhattan Gal had the year before.

In two successive years, their first in the Angus business, Gallagher's Stud had a National Heifer Champion and National Bull Champion. These genetics miracles had been purchased by a man whose initial motive was to buy an animal for his grandchildren's summer amusement.

By Angus breeders' standards, Gallagher's Stud's one hundred acres was a spot on the wall —nothing like the 40,000-acre Williams Farm the Brodys had visited in Montana in the past year. Marlene and Brody had met Jerry Williams at an Angus auction at the Erdman Farm in South Dakota. Williams, having taken a liking to the Brodys, invited them to see his farm. The fact that it was in Montana seemed an inconvenience to the Brodys but not to Williams, who had his large private jet parked nearby.

The weather on route was stormy and the descent through the mountains socked in with clouds and snow. Williams told the Brodys that the view of the surrounding mountains would be spectacular if only they were visible, but the bad weather detracted not at all from the beauty of the establishment Williams had created.

The Williams Farm living quarters were baronial: elegant and expensive. It might have been ready for a *Gentlemen's Quarterly* photo shoot. Williams had millions tied up in state of the art farm equipment. At the feed station, his cattle were hooked up to monitors so that computers could measure their feed intake. Compared with the Williams operation, Gallagher's Stud was minor league. And yet after only two years in business, Gallagher's Stud was sitting atop the pinnacle of the Angus world. Williams told the Brodys that he looked forward to seeing them again.

The year after the Brodys' visit to Montana, Williams bought a golf course in Connecticut, just a short drive from Gallagher's Stud. The next summer, Williams called Brody and Brody invited him, his wife, his son, grandson, daughter-in-law and wife to lunch at Gallagher's Stud and to take a tour of the farm. The group squeezed itself into the recently completed sunroom/dining room, and then the Brodys gave Williams a tour of the farm.

Close to a year passed, and when Brody next saw Williams, Williams told Brody that he had sold his Montana farm. He said that it was costing him $200,000 a month. And then he said, "When I saw your farm, I decided to sell mine."

Brody was reminded of a conversation he once had with the celebrated Angus breeder, Fred Johnson, who told Brody that each year he put in more money than he took out. Angus breeding was costing him a fortune. On a subsequent meeting, Brody asked, "Well, Fred, are you still putting in, or are you taking out?" Johnson's laconic reply was, "Putting in."

Apart from the prize ring, the fortunes of Gallagher's Stud

continued to soar. Patriot's semen brought in as much as $200,000 per year. The commercial and financial importance of a champion bull is enormous. The commercial population of Angus cattle in the United States alone is ninety million animals. And the vitality of this asset is dependent on the genetic enrichment provided by the registered Angus herd. A champion bull like Patriot is an essential part of this huge commercial enterprise. Tom Burke, longtime president of the American Angus Hall of Fame, was once asked why there was no jealousy of Brody in the light of his almost instant success in a business at which most Angus people had worked for years. Burke said, "A rising tide raises all ships." Gallagher's Stud was in flood tide.

Less happily, Manhattan Gal's offspring proved to be undersized. Brody, after having made a lucrative sale to some Canadian breeders, offered to return the money. The Canadians accepted his offer. However, a heifer which the Brodys thought as "the other heifer, 'Hedgerow's Jestress,'" turned out to have enduring breeding qualities and was the producer of champions.

These vagaries did not escape Brody's attention, and he would not be blinded by success. Brody took into account the ineradicable variables that yielded the disappointment of Manhattan Gal's offspring and the unexpected success of Hedgerow's Jestress. Brody's ability to select great cattle rested largely on the advice he received from Ira Boggs, Kevin O'Brien and Phil Trowbridge. It was crucial to the success of the entire operation that Brody trust the judgment of his key cattlemen. In the restaurant business Brody's ability to educate and train his key personnel and to give them support and discipline had been major reasons for his success. His ability to build, keep and nurture a management team had been at the core of Brody's success with Restaurant Associates. The core of Brody's management style is trust.

Although Brody can be a harsh taskmaster, he provides the

education and patience necessary to give his people the tools they need to excel. He expects them to make good use of what they have learned, and his trust is rarely disappointed. When an employee crosses Brody, Brody acts quickly and without remorse. But when the axe falls, he never gossips. The matter is laid to rest.

Phil Trowbridge was only twenty years old when he found Patriot. Even though the huge price Brody paid for the animal paid big dividends, Trowbridge still did not have full confidence in himself. The problem did not lie with Brody, but with Trowbridge, who admits to his lack of experience and his tendency to be awed by Brody's self-confidence and experience of the wider world. Trowbridge remembers one incident that he thinks reveals the essence of Brody's excellence as a manager.

In October 1977, Brody told Trowbridge to fly to Alberta, Canada to take a look at some registered Angus. He gave Trowbridge a checkbook and a credit card. Trowbridge, the smalltown farm boy, was overwhelmed. In Alberta, Trowbridge found a cow he thought Brody should buy. Over the phone, Brody told him he was free to make his own decisions. Trowbridge discovered the anxieties that go along with authority.

When Trowbridge returned to Gallagher's Stud, he met with Brody and said, "I *think* I bought a great cow today." "What did she cost?" asked Brody. "$7,500" was the reply. From Brody there was ominous silence. Trowbridge thought that he was about to have his head bitten off. Then Brody said, "I want to tell you something. If you only *think* you bought a great cow, I can have your bags sent to your dad's in Buffalo." Trowbridge said to himself what he should have said to Brody, "I *know* this is a great cow." From that time on, Trowbridge's decisions were voiced clearly, just the way the boss liked them.

Trowbridge was to become one of the most respected cattle

judges in the country and one of its best thoroughbred farm managers. He learned that the more he was confident of his own judgment, the more use he was to Brody. It would be the most *efficient* way for them to do business.

GMH Bluebird 17 E, the cow from Alberta, went on to become a very important breeder for Gallagher's Stud. By 1 9 7 8, Gallagher's Stud was a nationally recognized Angus farm, with over one hundred cows and visitors from around the world. Big business interests from Argentina and Germany made the farm feel a bit like corporate America. In the light of all the awards and acclaim, it would have been quite easy for the owner of Gallagher's Stud to let himself believe that he was running an economically sensible business. In the midst of all the acclaim and the apparent success, Brody decided to submit the Angus operation to economic analysis.

Brody requested the National Association of Angus Breeders to look at the vital statistics of Gallagher's Stud. Brody wanted to know when an operation like his, of its specific size and with its operating costs, could expect to make a profit. The carefully thought out reply came back from the National Association: Gallagher's Stud in all likelihood would never make a profit.

On January 1, 1979, after two years of unparalleled national success as a breeder of champions, Brody called a meeting. He told O'Brien and Trowbridge that Gallagher's Stud was getting out of the Angus business. Unlike Fred Johnson, Brody was not willing to see the days of "paying out" become a lifelong scenario.

As bowled over by Brody's announcement as Trowbridge was, it did not entirely surprise him. That summer legislation had been approved which gave the New York Thoroughbred Breeding and Development Fund money to be made available not only for the betterment of the breed in New York State but also to encourage jobs and the preservation of green spaces left fallow by the declining New York State dairy industry. Trowbridge was aware that Brody found the money, which would be available to New York State breeders, attractive.

During Thanksgiving of 1978 on a trip back to his parents' home, Trowbridge had confided to his father that something was awry at the farm. Trowbridge told his father that he thought he was going to lose his job. The idea was crushing. His father heard him out and asked, "Are you flexible?" At first Trowbridge did not get his father's drift. His father then said, "Would you mind working with horses? Because that's what he is going to do. Mr. Brody is going to ask you to work with the horses." Trowbridge did not believe him. But his father was right.

The word of Brody's decision was instantly known in the Angus business. Trowbridge had no idea what his work for Gallagher's Stud had done for his reputation all over the country. That week Trowbridge's phone rang with several good job offers from all over the country. He even interviewed for one.

The job of managing the horses might have gone to Kevin O'Brien, who, after all, had served Brody well. Indeed, Kevin's father had made an offer for Brody's whole herd. Brody said that he would take the offer under consideration. While mulling over this proposition, Brody learned that Kevin O'Brien had offered the job of managing the herd to Phil Trowbridge. That would have left Brody without any managers for Gallagher's Stud and Brody did not choose to offer his herd up for slaughter. At that point Brody offered the job of managing Gallagher's Stud to Phil Trowbridge, who accepted. Trowbridge would not only manage the horses, but also keep the herd intact.

Manhattan Gal Redux

In the thoroughbred horse business, if a breeder is fortunate enough to acquire a good mare, he must wait about three years to see his good fortune bear fruit on the racetrack. In the meantime, he pays bills. The new direction in which Brody was taking Gallagher's Stud would require a great deal of patience, risk, bill paying, and courage

Those who know Brody well, especially those who work for him, would not list patience as one of his dominant characteristics. When Brody wants something done and he asks that one of his employees do it, no matter how civilly the request is made (and it invariably is), it is totally clear that he expects it to be done right away. No response other than obedience is required or expected. If Brody wants work to begin on a barn or to have a fence erected or to get a lawyer's opinion or to get a plane reservation, he means right away. But that does not mean that Brody is not willing to wait. Brody is a realist—above all, a realist—and one thing he learned from the prize Angus business is that the breeder had the hardest job but the biggest reward. Breeding takes patience.

In the thoroughbred horse racing business, there are two timelines to success. The quick route is to buy a winner. The second route is to breed winners. Brody chose to become a breeder, though, of course, the desire to stand in the winner's circle with a Grade 1 champion was alluring. The choice to concentrate on breeding and broodmares in particular was not entirely his. He could not, with a sheik-like wave of his check book, buy his way into the big-time racing circles. He would have to make use of what he had already learned in the cattle business, while educating himself with more than a little help from his friends.

Although Brody decided to focus his energies on horses, he did not give up his Angus business, only its show circuit aspect. However, with Trowbridge maintaining the herd, in addition to his burgeoning horse responsibilities, in the course of the next few years, Gallagher's Stud prepared for the dispersal sale and built a sale barn for that purpose.

In September 1987, the dispersal sale at the new show barn was a much anticipated event in the entire Angus community. Brody arranged to have it lavishly catered by the Grand Central Oyster Bar and Gallagher's Steakhouse. More than $1 million worth of cattle was sold at a record average of $13,000 per animal.

The following October, when the stock market plunged precipitously, several purchasers of Gallagher's Stud's cattle accused Brody of insider's knowledge. Brody had had no such amazing foresight. His decision to sell was based on his unsentimental assessment of the economics facing the Stud were it to remain in the Angus business. Ironically, Brody was soon to discover that replacing the economic impracticalities of the Angus business with the long odds and slow payback of the thoroughbred breeding business, did little if anything to diminish his risk.

Brody began his search for a handhold in the thoroughbred business at Gallagher's Steakhouse, where he had a conversation with the head bartender who, like many of the restaurant's clients, was a lifelong gambler and follower of the ponies. Brody, whose research is always thorough and conducted with no sparing of expense or effort, figured that the Guys and Dolls world of Gallagher's, where bookies and track aficionados had gathered for decades, was a homey but practical place to start.

Brody asked the bartender for the name of the "best trainer in New York" and after conferring with one of his waiters, the head bartender cited Phil Johnson. Bartender and waiter volunteered to contact Johnson on Brody's behalf through one of their acquaintances who was the head of security at Belmont.

True to their word, they arranged a meeting between Brody and Johnson, and after Johnson checked out Brody's credentials, he asked Brody how he wanted to get started. Brody suggested that a good way would be for them to buy a racehorse. When Johnson asked how much money Brody wanted to spend, Brody suggested $30,000. Johnson, did not seem overly impressed by the number but said that he would try. After several weeks, he had come up with nothing. He told Brody that he had selected a certain horse, but that when he had had it vetted, it had failed to pass muster.

By now it was summertime and Brody still did not have a horse. Johnson told Brody that at the Saratoga racing meeting there would be a special sale of New York State thoroughbreds. With the recent legislative money voted to promote New York thoroughbreds now available to owners of New York horses, Saratoga seemed like an economical place to look.

Johnson recommended that the Brodys buy a colt. However, the Brodys had learned from the cattle business that the breeding business lay with the mare. In the cattle business you could buy the semen from any bull or season to any bull, but you needed the cow to get a decent product. To buy a yearling colt whose payoff, if any, would be at the track, would serve almost no purpose. Gallagher's Stud would be better served with a mare.

Of all the animals they saw at Saratoga, Marlene most fancied a filly. Brody telephoned Johnson and asked him to examine the filly Marlene had selected, but Johnson disapproved, saying that the filly would have hoof and leg problems.

At the sale itself, the Brody's relative unimportance in Johnson's estimation was visibly demonstrated when they were being seated at the end of the row of Phil Johnson's more established clients. When the colt that Johnson had recommended was shown, Brody said to Marlene "We'll have to pay our dues," figuring that going along with Johnson's recommendation would demonstrate that they were willing to learn from the person they had, after all, hired because of his superior knowledge and experience. Even though Brody bought the colt mostly to placate Johnson, Marlene's instinctual admiration of the filly was strong, and when the filly was offered for sale, Brody bought her too. They paid $10,000 and they named her "Manhattan Gal," hoping that history would repeat itself.

Manhattan Gal and the colt were shipped to Florida for the winter to be broken and to start their training. It would be the first season in which Brody had horses in training, but because he needed to be in New York to attend to the restaurants, he would learn of the horses's progress only through long distance telephone calls.

Johnson called Brody from sunny Florida to tell him that he had decided that the horses should do some swimming as part of their conditioning program. Meanwhile, in New York, it was snowing and the slush in the streets was up to Brody's ankles. Outside Gallagher's, on his way back to his Central Park South apartment, Brody waved futilely for a cab. He arrived back at the apartment tired, cold, and wet. He took off his rubbers, his hat, and his overcoat, and said to Marlene, "What kind of system is this in which I have two horses who are swimming in Florida and here I am freezing in New York and covered in slush?"

The filly came to Belmont at the age of three, and in her first race, finished in the back of the pack. Phil Johnson, implying his disdain for Brody's having bought the filly in the first place, recommended that Manhattan Gal be sent to Finger Lakes, a secondary track in New York State where he would put her under the supervision of trainer José Triana, a Cuban who spoke only Spanish. The Brodys need not worry about the language barrier Johnson claimed, because Johnson had an assistant who spoke Spanish, and Johnson would be able to stay on top of things from his base in New York.

Fortunately, Brody also had an assistant who knew about horses and who also spoke Spanish—Marlene, the professional interpreter. Marlene was to prove over the years an extremely acute judge of thoroughbreds. She developed an encyclopedic knowledge of racing lines and an eye that invariably spotted quality. Marlene became the communicator with José Triana, the Cuban trainer. Triana loved the looks of Manhattan Gal, but recommended that this "beautiful horse" needed to be" fired" in order to repair some damage to her leg bones. Brody agreed, at that point in his equine education, not knowing what "firing" meant.

As Manhattan Gal entered into serious training. Triana's enthusiasm continued to grow, and Manhattan Gal went on to win $150,000 including stakes races. The colt which Johnson had recommended amounted to nothing.

As Manhattan Gal the heifer had done in Angus competition, Manhattan Gal the filly did in thoroughbred racing—she launched the Brodys into the winners' circle with great expectations that there were more good things to come. But, like her

Angus namesake, the equine Manhattan Gal proved to be a disappointment as a broodmare.

Manhattan Gal's success at the track was rewarding, but her poor performance as a broodmare served to remind Brody of the central importance he must give to breeding characteristics in mares if Gallagher's Stud was to remain a viable business. If that could be achieved, only then would he stand a chance of succeeding at the more costly and more risky enterprise of acquiring racing champions.

Meanwhile back at the farm, Phil Trowbridge was engaged in building three barns at once, while installing miles of fences and various mandatory safety features. To prepare him for the task of barn building, Brody sent the 22-year old Trowbridge to Maryland and Kentucky to inspect the best that those thorough-bred capitals had to offer.

While Trowbridge was scouting in Maryland and Kentucky, Brody and Marlene traveled in Europe, studying barns in England and visiting in Italy the stud of Federico Tesio, the breeder of the champions Nearco and Ribot. Brody traveled to Ireland with warm and influential introductions from E. Barry Ryan, horseman and Irish-American gentleman of infinite charm, who set up educational trips to various Irish and English farms.

In particular, Brody was impressed with the barns at Windfields in Canada, owned by E. P. Taylor, who had bred Northern Dancer, the stallion with the greatest influence on thoroughbred racing in the modern era. Brody used them as a model for the barns at Gallagher's Stud. In only his first year in the thoroughbred business, Brody was already embarked in creating a state-of-the art stud farm, which would be as efficient as any in the world. Just as with his entry into the Angus business, Brody assumed that only the most advanced techniques and the most thorough research would yield acceptable results.

Brody and Trowbridge were in constant communication about the progress of the building program. The barns were at the center of their concerns. Above all they must be efficient. Brody worked out a hub design in which the barns were at the center with paddocks fanning out from them. The utility of the hub design was driven home to Trowbridge by his study of linear barns in Kentucky, where concerns about the picturesque conflicted with efficient planning. The field hands made a ten-minute's walk to the fields and then back to the paddock four times a day. At Gallagher's Stud, the longest walk was thirty seconds.

Phil Johnson was still Brody's trainer in November 1979, when they attended the Keenland broodmare sale and bought three mares. Because Trowbridge was busy building the barns, Brody's three mares were wintered at the Rojan farm about 15 miles from Gallagher's Stud, where they birthed the first Gallagher's Stud foals.

Once again, Brody was off to a fast start, for the colt among the first foals turned out to be Master Digby, who would go on to have a splendid career at the races. Brody decided to place Master Digby with a new trainer, Howie Tesher and under Tesher, Master Digby became a consistent winner. Master Digby gave the Brodys their first taste of the excitement and elegance of the world of successful thoroughbred owners, and it stimulated the Brodys to cast their eyes to European thoroughbred racing and its fabled venues such as Epsom Downs and Longchamps.

Gallagher's Stud's commercial breeding program had gone into high gear. That program would remain the commercial mainstay of the farm, but the ideal would be the combination of the breeding program with the development of champion race horses—horses which would compete in Europe at the thoroughbred world's most elegant venues.

In 1980 the fourth barn was constructed for broodmares, and

Brody started traveling in Europe, acquainting himself with English and French bloodstock and evaluating the best of the European trainers. He made the acquaintance of François Boutin and Guy Harwood, two great trainers, who would be influential in the affairs of Gallagher's Stud.

Boutin was introduced to the Brodys when Marlene became the chairperson of a celebrated tribute to Josephine Baker. Boutin belonged to that class of highly-educated French trainers, who are in fact entrepreneurs, running the entire business of the stable, not just working with the horses. Unlike their American counterparts, who rarely get past high school and whose responsibilities begin and end with the horses they train, many European trainers are part of the social scene that includes the owners of the horses they train.

Among the persons working on the tribute to Baker was Solange Gaussen, the wife of Gérard Gaussen, then the Consul General of France in New York. As the friendship between the Gaussens and the Brodys developed, after the Gaussens had visited Gallagher's Stud, the Brodys proposed that the two families join together in the owning of a French horse.

Solange Gaussen, who otherwise loved horses, protested. The Brodys discovered that her family had been deeply involved with French racing and that they had lost millions. Undoubtedly, thought the Brodys, this was the source of her reluctance. In order to keep them in the picture while eliminating their risk, Brody offered the Gaussens ten percent of the winnings of their first horse, Moonlight Serenade. In return the Brodys were introduced to Solange Gaussen's uncle's trainer. He was François Boutin.

The relationship with Boutin flourished. On one visit to Gallagher's Stud, Boutin told Brody that he would like to get into the restaurant business. Brody told Boutin that whenever he felt the urge to get into the restaurant business, he should lie down and wait for it to go away.

In addition to his ongoing care and expert advice, Boutin asked Brody to supply him with the charts of all the bloodlines of the horses at Gallagher's Stud. Boutin would study them and make his recommendations, one of which led to Brody's purchase of Moonlight Serenade, who became a successful broodmare for Gallagher's Stud. Brody who remembered the short shrift given him by his first trainer, Phil Johnson, was impressed.

Brody would have liked to continue his relationship with Boutin, but Boutin was offered and accepted the position of training Stavros Niarchos's horses. Adorable Micol, by then the most precocious horse in the Gallagher's Stud stable, was turned over to the care of Boutin's assistant, Jean de Roualle, who eventually campaigned Adorable Micol in France with great success.

In 1983 Master Digby was named a division champion of the New York Racing Association and was on a path to take his place among the premier racehorses in America. With a crop of promising foals waiting in the wings, there was a rosy glow over the racing fortunes of Gallagher's Stud.

The Brodys attended Belmont to watch Master Digby, under the ride of Angel Cordero, compete for another stakes victory. The anticipation was just the kind of excitement that the Brodys had dreamed of, but had rightly believed was a long shot to attain. Two furlongs out of the gate, Master Digby suddenly stopped and Cordero leaped from the saddle. Cordero had heard a loud snap; Master Digby had shattered his sesemoid bone, reducing it almost to rubble. Master Digby had to be euthanized.

Master Digby always had a special place in the hearts of Gallagher's Stud. He had come from the first foals produced by the farm; the effect on Brody and Marlene was deep. Their responsibility for their horses went far beyond the horses' value as a business proposition.

From the very start, Brody kept Gallagher's Stud in the forefront of veterinary care and he never spared any expense, even in the face of the most pessimistic medical predictions. This single-minded dedication led to some medical miracles, in which animals given up as deformed or incurable were nursed back to health and to championship performances that no one outside the farm believed were possible. Unfortunately, Master Digby's success as the first champion of the first foals born at Gallagher's Stud would be forever linked to his tragic demise.

In 1982 Brody bought two mares that would produce great champions. Turn-to-Me by Cyane would produce Adorable Micol by Riverman. Why Me Lord would produce Allez Milord by Tom Rolfe. The fruits of these mares would become apparent in 1987, the best year for Gallagher's Stud, with Adorable Micol and Allez Milord winning big in Europe and America, fulfilling the Brodys' dreams of international success.

Adorable Micol turned out to be the most influential mare in the Gallagher's Stud. As a baby, she was so nearly perfect that everyone was infatuated by her, including Phil Trowbridge. Her bloodlines were impeccable. And by the time she was a broodmare, Trowbridge dubbed her "a blue hen," meaning that when bred properly, she would be able do what ever she wanted. However, her perfect start turned painful after three months, when her front feet began to toe out so badly that she was in danger of hurting herself if let out of the stall.

Many owners would have given up on and written her off to bad luck, but Brody told Trowbridge to do whatever it would take to mend her. Trowbridge kept her closed up in her stall and took weekly pictures of her feet. He constantly stood her on a board and traced her feet configuration in order to monitor her progress. Every day the Brodys were at the farm, they visited with

Adorable Micol at least twice a day. Eventually, with Phil Trowbridge's daily ministrations, Adorable Micol grew healthy and the champion strutted her stuff on the track and as a productive broodmare.

Allez Milord

Bold Reasoning had earned his reputation as a great race horse. He had set the record for six furlongs at Belmont, which still stood. Brody's inspection of racing bloodlines made him determined to own a Bold Reasoning mare, Why Me Lord, who was in foal to Tom Rolfe. Tom Rolfe had won the Preakness.

Phil Trowbridge could understand the genetic attractiveness of Why Me Lord, but he was shocked by how pigeon-toed she was. Trowbridge invited Dr. Jim Beldon, a world-renowned veterinarian, to the barn, and asked what he thought of Why Me Lord. Dr. Beldon said, "Get rid of her."

Fortunately, the Brodys kept Why Me Lord and she gave them a colt by Tom Rolfe called Allez Milord, who went on to win more than $700,000 and was sold to a Japanese syndicate for $1.3 million.

At the 1983 Keenland sale Brody had put a very modest reserve of $50,000 on Allez Milord, and fully expected him to be sold. Since his fee as a stallion had been established at $40,000 the reserve of $50,000 was indeed designed to achieve a certain sale. Nonetheless, Allez Milord did not sell and so the Brodys brought him home. They were disappointed.

The following November, the Brodys went to the Fasig-Tipton breeding stock sale in Lexington, Kentucky. There was an important broodmare, Morning Games, for sale, who was the dam of Alphabatim. Alphabatim had just missed being the two-year old English Champion.

Brody faced a crucial strategic decision in 1987. It had taken 1982's broodmares five years to produce the crop of 1987. Brody was eager to have a racing champion, but recognized that to produce one out of his own mares not only involved at least five years, but also the strong possibility that no champion would be forthcoming, despite the most carefully planned crosses. In five years Brody would be in his early 70's. Knowing that Brody was eager for racing success, Trowbridge suggested that Brody buy some yearling fillies out of the best possible breedings, train them, race them, and then retire them to breed. Brody listened carefully to Trowbridge, and said, "Young man, I do not have the time." Gallagher's Stud would continue to stress the continuity of its broodmares, if for no other reason than that there seemed to be no other choice. Brody knew that something unexpected would have to happen in order for him to develop or acquire a champion. But there was a great surprise waiting in the paddocks of Gallagher's Stud. Happily for the Brodys, that unattractive yearling, who three years earlier no one wanted to buy at Keenland, Allez Milord, was soon to become the world-class male champion for whom the Brodys had so long awaited.

In the sunlight of a perfect November day, Morning Games, white and impressively configured, caught the attention of Marlene, who exclaimed at her beauty. Brody and Trowbridge agreed. As the Brodys stood outside the Fasig-Tipton sales pavilion, the blood stock agent, Eugenio Colombo, came over to the Brodys and said, "You've got to buy that mare because she is the dam of Alphabatim, who is going to be a world champion."

The last couple of years had been economically kind to Brody. In 1974, during the negotiations with the Metropolitan Transit Authority, the landlords of the Grand Central Oyster Bar, Brody had met Stan Lewis, the head of its real estate operations. After he had departed the MTA, Lewis, who had come to admire Brody, asked him to join in a real estate venture. Brody pointed out to Lewis the opportunity to purchase a relatively low-rise building very close to Gallagher's Steakhouse. Lewis and Brody were able to buy the building through a mortgage provided by the seller. Subsequently, they were able to sell the building to a new customer under terms which would provide Brody with an instant cash flow in the millions. These added funds would enable Brody not only to buy more expensive thoroughbreds, but also to finance the purchase of his world class charter yachts Bonheur 1 and her successor, Bonheur 2.

Armed with the wealth to back his desires, Brody, who was very fond of Eugenio Colombo, let Colombo bid for Morning Games on behalf of Gallagher's Stud. Brody stopped his bidding at $500,000. The winning bid was $540,000. Colombo hurried from the auction tent and returned shortly to report that the winning bidder was Nelson Bunker Hunt—as in Texas oil, cattle, and silver—and that Hunt had told Colombo that he had not known that Colombo was the underbidder. If Colombo wanted the horse, Hunt had magnanimously said, "Take her."

When Colombo reported that Hunt was willing to step aside, Brody wondered what was it that Hunt had found out that made him willing to bow out? Somehow Hunt's warmth of heart was not convincing. However, putting his enthusiasm before his skepticism, Brody bought Morning Games for $540,000, who returned considerably more than one million dollars to Gallagher's Stud as a broodmare.

Owning Morning Games gave Brody a substantial reason to

inspect her progeny, most particularly, Alphabatim, who was being trained in England by Guy Harwood, who Brody wanted to train Allez Milord. Brody felt that Allez Milord's configuration was similar to the type favored by Harwood, and that if he could get Harwood's attention, Harwood might find training Allez Milord a good fit.

The Brodys traveled to England and visited Harwood in order to see Alphabatim at first hand. They inspected Harwood's other horses and learned more of Harwood as a trainer. Later that summer, when Allez Milord returned to Gallagher's Stud, Brody was convinced that the horse had the kind of appearance that Hardwood liked, a little bit long—"covers a piece of ground"—as the British say.

That August at Saratoga, Brody saw Harwood and invited him to come to Gallagher's Stud to evaluate Allez Milord. Harwood pleaded that he was too busy as he was leaving for England almost immediately. He did condescend, however, to send one of his associates, Amanda Skiffington, a blood stock agent, to look at the yearling Allez Milord.

Skiffington seemed entranced by Gallagher's Stud and by Allez Milord. She was effusive in her admiration for the horse and for the farm. Brody expected that she would convey her positive impressions to Harwood.

However, time passed, and Brody heard nothing from Harwood. Finally, Brody phoned Harwood directly and Harwood reported that Skiffington had told him that Allez Milord was not the kind of horse that Harwood would want to train. Brody was so shocked that he said nothing.

The next time Brody saw Harwood was at the September sale at Keenland. Harwood's initial rejection or indifference had not dimmed Brody's desire to have Harwood as a trainer. Brody set out to seduce him. Brody had observed that almost no one could resist the lure of being offered a lift in a private jet, and, since there were no direct airplane connections from Lexington to Kennedy, Brody offered to charter a little jet, and fly Harwood to the farm. While Harwood was looking over Allez Milord, Brody would order the jet to stand by awaiting Harwood's orders to take him to Kennedy. Harwood found the offer irresistible.

Harwood stared at Allez Milord's profile for quite a long time. Then, with no great enthusiasm, he said to Brody, "Well, you're the owner; if you want me to train him I'll train him." Thus with such lukewarm acquiescence, did Harwood undertake the training of Allez Milord who was soon to set the European racing world ablaze.

Allez Milord at two, won his first race on October 17, 1985, Brody's birthday. As a three-year old under Harwood in England, Allez Milord won the the Schroder Predominate, a prep race for the Epsom Derby. He remained undefeated and went into the Epsom Derby as the second favorite. Adorable Micol was winning in France, and won several other races. Gallagher's Stud had become an important force in Europe. It was just what the Brodys had aimed for.

At about this time, Harwood reported to Brody that an Arab horse owner had offered more than $2 million for a sixty percent share of Allez Milord. His value on the thoroughbred market was rocketing upward. Not only would the Brodys benefit from a lucrative sale, so would the trainer, Harwood, who was in for a piece of the sales price.

Brody was all for selling him, but after spending many hours explaining to Marlene what that kind of money would mean to their financial condition, Brody listened to Marlene maintain that the prospect of Allez Milord's winning the Derby was too exciting. Would they ever be in that position again? And how could they walk away from their horse and watch it race in someone else's colors?

Brody was delighted that Marlene had restored him to his senses. Of course, they would keep Allez Milord and race him in the colors of Gallagher's Stud. Unfortunately, Allez Milord received a serious leg injury from bumping in the course of the Derby and finished in the middle of the pack. After recovering for two months, Allez Milord returned to the track and was victorious. The Brodys shipped Allez Milord to Germany where he won the Puma Europa Prize in Cologne, making him "Champion of Germany." In November, Allez Milord was shipped to Japan to run in the Japan Cup where he finished second by a nose.

Allez Milord began his four-year old campaign with a victory, but in his second race at Sandown, the Gordon Richards Grade 3, Mtoto, who would go on to win the Arc De Triomphe, beat him. Brody would later discover that Allez Milord had bled. Harwood did not tell Brody.

At that point, Terry Yoshida of Japan, a member of Japan's most influential horse-owning family, made a new offer for Allez Milord. The offer was for $1.3 million, and the Brodys would be entitled to keep one-half the prize money Allez Milord might win for the rest of the year. The Brodys sold Allez Milord to Yoshida and agreed to manage the horse for the rest of the year.

Well into the next year, Allez Milord was shipped to Belmont to run in the Turf Classic, where the Yoshidas had traveled to see their new acquisition. Allez Milord finished far back in the pack, having bled profusely after having led by ten lengths.

That evening, in order to dispel their gloom, the Brodys invited the Yoshidas to dine with them at Gallagher's. The Yoshidas were charming and upbeat. They were leaving New York the next day to continue on their travels. There had been expectations that Allez Milord would return to Europe for the rest of the year and then take one more shot at the Japan Cup before his retirement.

Later that night, in a conversation with Harwood, Brody discovered that Allez Milord had bled for the first time at Sandown. The next day, Brody telephoned Harwood and suggested that they not send the horse back to England—that they take him instead to California, where horses can run on Lasix, a medication which helps control lung bleeding. Harwood asked for twenty-four hours. He arranged for John Gosden to do the training. Brody tried to reach the Yoshida to tell him about the change of plans for Allez Milord, but he could not reach him.

The Brodys organized the transportation and shipped Allez Milord to California; there he smoked the field to win $250,000 and the Grade 1 Oak Tree Invitational under a great ride by Chris McCarron. The Yoshidas could hardly object to a change of plans that had led to such a triumph.

Brody kept Allez Milord in Lasix-friendly California and ran him next in the Breeders Cup. The Yoshidas, eager to view their champion, needed twenty-two tickets for their investor operation. But there was to be no celebration. Allez Milord was now passed his peak.

The Yoshidas then took him home. That was the end of his racing career.

Bonheur

Nobody needs *a yacht* —Jerome Brody

The sizeable profit realized in the real estate deal partnered with Stan Lewis allowed Brody to make the winning bid for Morning Games; that investment repaid Brody's initial investment twice over. About the same time as the Morning Games acquisition, Brody's newly deepened pockets opened another investment horizon in the world of chartered yachts. It seemed a chance to combine business and pleasure.

The Brodys were accustomed to spending several weekends of the winter months in southern Florida. Brody felt that a yacht would give them the freedom to sail from club to club and would get him back onto the ocean, which he loved so much.

As always, when entering a new field, Brody did some research. He found a sea captain and polished salesman, Nigel Helps, to indoctrinate him in the qualities of yachts and in the entire business of chartering. Help's description of the charter business made Brody think that it had several strong similarities to the restaurant business. Both were hospitality businesses and the success of both relied on the efficacy of key personnel.

In both businesses, keeping key personnel was as difficult as it was essential. In the world of chartering, women members of the crew were invariably overqualified: their real aim being marital rather than nautical. They would leave when they found a suitable partner. The men, on the other hand, were usually underqualified, and since that created a demand for men with good reputations and solid credentials among an ever-growing number of yacht owners, an owner could lose his best male crew to a better offer at any time. A strong captain with his pulse on the state of the labor market and the loyalty of his crew was essential. He would be as important to chartering as Austin Cox had been to the restaurants.

Two days after meeting Helps, Brody invited him to lunch and said he was agreeable to having Helps find him a yacht, but that Helps, himself, would have to be the captain, at least until Brody had gotten some primary schooling. Helps found the offer attractive. By the end of the meeting, Brody had calculated that it would take only twenty weeks of charter business a year to make the operation go.

Helps went right to work and found Brody a suitable boat. Brody made a substantial deposit only to find out that the owner of the yacht had already sold the boat to another person. He refused to return Brody's deposit and Brody was forced to sue.

At the trial, the attorney for the defendant, as part of his defense strategy, thought it important to demonstrate that Brody wanted the yacht for investment purposes. He looked accusingly at Brody and asked, "Mr. Brody, didn't you *need* this yacht?" Brody responded, "No one *needs* a yacht." At which point the defense attorney, a roly-poly Southerner said, "I object, your Honor, everyone needs a yacht!" causing even the judge to break out into laughter.

Brody got his money back, but not for long. The charter boat business would see to that.

A few months later, Captain Helps called Brody from France

to report that he had found him a boat of suitable size and condition. It was now moored in the harbor of La Napoule, France. The Brodys flew over to look at it and they liked what they saw. Brody asked the owners for a cruise around the harbor. Brody, who had never been behind the wheel of so large a boat and who was unfamiliar with the waters in which he was motoring, got behind the wheel, while Marlene kept her fingers crossed.

After the test drive, Brody made an offer for the boat, even though he knew it would require work. Brody had made so low an offer that he believed it would be refused, but it was not. Adding to the attraction of the selling price was the advantageous position of the US dollar, then at the height of its purchase power in relation to the franc, which was struggling economically under Premier François Mitterand. For the time being, Bonheur was a bargain.

The interior design, dominated by black and orange, was to Brody's eyes, extremely ugly. But after undergoing some structural re-designing and rehab work in the United States, the newly rechristened Bonheur was ready for pleasure and, hopefully, for the charter business.

The Brodys grew to love Bonheur, although their personal use was limited by IRS regulations to two weeks per year; and the twenty weeks per year of charter time was never achieved. Brody found an excellent new captain for Bonheur, Mark Ellis. The Brodys snorkeled in the Caribbean and cruised the coastlines of the Mediterranean. They entertained their friends, and, of course, saw that the superbly disciplined staff served them the best food and wine. But, when Brody received an offer for Bonheur that would yield him a substantial profit, he accepted. To continue operating Bonheur with its negative cash flow would soon wipe out the benefits of the bargain price for which she was acquired.

It was not, however, easy to forget the pleasures of owning a luxury yacht. For the next two years, when the Brodys wanted to vacation on a yacht, they chartered one for themselves and their friends. On one of these charters, Blair Albert was the captain. Soon, Brody's desire to own a yacht was rekindled. This time he would make certain it was a masterpiece and that would be due in large part to the talents and energy of Blair Albert.

Albert was charming, attractive, and athletic. During the period between Bonheurs, Albert had been the Brodys' charter captain and a friendship was struck. Albert was a magnificent captain. He had been an air traffic controller when Ronald Reagan had fired them for their illegal strike, and then Albert had turned to the sea. He was a master diver, pilot, and sky diver. He played guitar, was charming to the guests, and had boundless energy, always game to take the Brodys' guests on a mountain hike or a sightseeing expedition, Brody asked him to sign on as the captain of Bonheur 2 and to supervise her design and construction. Albert and the Brodys traveled to Sweden and Italy before giving the job of constructing Bonheur 2 to a Portland, Oregon boatyard.

Bonheur 2 would be two and a half years in construction, and Brody credits Albert, who was on site during the entire period, with full credit for the success of Bonheur 2.

Bonheur 2 was a 130-foot long luxury yacht, which had five cabins and sailed with a crew of seven. It would eventually be voted by *Showboats* magazine the best new charter yacht in the world. Not only was Bonheur 2 excellently engineered and designed, but its interior spaces and accouterments—furniture, paintings, rugs, bathroom fixtures—were personally selected by the Brodys with the same care to aesthetics and quality that had been given to the Four Seasons, La Fonda del Sol and L'Étoile.

Getting Bonheur 2 built to Brody's specifications turned out to be difficult and unpleasant. The Portland builder set himself against anything that to him seemed extraordinary. When Brody suggested that a set of fold-down steps, which would enable guests to enter the water directly from the fantail, be designed, the builder balked and called the idea "stupid." The steps were built and were a great success.

During one of his numerous transcontinental visits to the Portland boatyard, Brody noticed two large, upright forms, which ran from the upper to the lower deck. He asked the builder if they were necessary, since they interfered with the design. He said that they could easily be done away with, and without saying anything more on the subject, had them removed. He then submitted a bill for $35,000. Removing the supports, he said, made additional structural work necessary. The dispute wound up in arbitration.

Brody designed a dining enclave for the upper deck. It was understood that the added cost of the construction would be Brody's. However, the builder, in the construction of other yachts subsequent to his work on Bonheur 2, appropriated Brody's design without his permission and without a fee. Another arbitration ensued. It was a welcome end to unpleasantness when, finally, Bonheur 2 was ready to sail. Brody considered her the most beautiful yacht ever put together.

Brody's main purpose had been to enjoy Bonheur 2 with Marlene and friends, while sailing to some of the most beautiful spots on earth. He never dreamed of using Bonheur 2 to mingle with the leisured rich and titled elite. When he accepted membership in the Monaco Yacht Club, it was solely because it was a helpful marina. And, despite the fact that Bonheur 2 in its splendid beauty was voted the best new charter boat in the world, Brody did not aspire to the top of the yachting world, which, like the world of thoroughbred racing, was inhabited by Arab sheiks and their billions. Bonheur 2 gave full reign to Brody's capacity to be a generous host.

Bonheur's first cruise was to the Sea of Cortez and down through the Panama Canal. Brody's business plan was to have the Bonheur sail the Caribbean in the winter and to be in Europe for the summer.

On trips to the historic sites of Greece and Turkey, to the south Atlantic and to the scuba and diving paradise of the Caribbean, the Brodys enjoyed themselves mightily and so did their friends. Aboard Bonheur 2, there were many places to sit in virtual isolation, which is rare for a yacht and which was a complement to the conviviality. By fax and satellite phone, Brody kept an eye on business back on the mainland, but not so anyone would notice. Captain and crew had their orders carefully written out each day. There was a plan for eating, swimming, diving, and sightseeing. And always the easy alternative was to do nothing, but sun or read or sleep.

In addition to the Brodys' own stateroom, there were four guest staterooms, each with its own marble bathroom shower stocked with lotions, soaps, conditioners, and shampoos from Paris. The television in each stateroom was equipped with a VCR and stocked with first run movies and classics. Each stateroom had a view of the ocean and its own telephone. First-time guests were astonished to discover that each time they left their room, even if only for a few minutes, one of the staff sneaked in to smooth the bed or to change the towels. It became a challenge to see if one could catch the staff in the act.

Breakfast was served on the canopied fantail of Bonheur 2, on a round table laden with silver, freshly laundered napkins, and a floral centerpiece. Rolls and bread were freshly baked, omelets prepared to order, and always there were various break-fast meats and cereals. Large platters of fresh fruit decorated with ferns pleased the eye as well as the palate. Anytime that a guest felt like a dip in the ocean, all he needed to do was to slip out of his seat and walk down the steps that Brody had built on the stern, directly into the water.

The main salon of Bonheur was 22 feet wide and 35 feet long, glassed in on all sides with tinted sloping glass and furnished with masterpieces of modern furniture design. It was here that liveried staff served formal dinners by candlelight. The dishes were the equal of Brody's greatest restaurants and the surroundings their superior. The interior walls of the hallways and passages were complexly inlaid with tropical woods and hung with the brilliant colors of Wallace Ting and Sam Francis.

The second deck, where luncheon was served *al fresco*, also housed the aquatic toys of Bonheur: two wave runners, jet skis and two powerboats loaded on and off by winch. The engine room housed a full array of scuba and deep diving equipment.

Over this entire luxurious enterprise Brody was delighted to have such a captain as Blair Albert. The Brodys had ordered Bonheur 2 to the vicinity of St. Martin's and Antigua. They had only a short time left for themselves before they were obligated to turn Bonheur 2 over to a charter leaving from Antigua. As a special treat to the Brodys, Albert insisted on taking the Bonheur into a small cove off the volcanic island of Saba. The waters surrounding Saba dive precipitously into the sea. Anchorage would be a problem, and, in fact, anchoring in the cove Albert had selected was forbidden.

Albert put Bonheur 2 stern to into the cove, planning to tie it up to something substantial on shore. As the bow of the boat was on the port side of the cove, Albert released the port anchor and swung the bow to the other side. The 300 feet of anchor chain ran all the way out and was lost. Albert was able to drop the starboard anchor on to a place which held.

In order to save face over losing the anchor in a cove he should not have been in in the first place, he told Brody that Albert and his first mate would dive for the lost anchor. Brody argued with him and told him not to go—that it was too dangerous. Besides the danger to Albert's own life, what would those aboard the Bonheur 2 do if anything should happen to its captain and first mate? But Albert's machismo swept aside Brody's opposition.

Albert and Joey, the first mate, would take an extra bottle of oxygen with them and a "lift bag," which they would attach to the lost anchor. When they inflated the lift bag from an extra air bottle, the anchor would float towards the surface. The engineer would accompany the two divers, hovering above them with an extra bottle of oxygen.

The men were diving in what they thought was 120 feet of water. Brody and the rest of the crew were pinned to the rail. Marlene had snorkeled over to where the bubbles were rising to the surface. After a half hour, the extra air bottle, meant to fill the lift bag, came to the surface, which seemed to indicate that things were going as scheduled. However, the air bag was followed shortly thereafter by the engineer. He had lost contact with Albert, and after fifteen minutes of searching, he was running out of air and could wait no longer.

The reality of the tragedy was too unbelievable. Brody was certain that Albert would appear somewhere down the shore, but Albert never did. Brody was on the phone and the radio to everyone who might be able to help. A nearby ship had professional deep-sea divers aboard. They responded immediately. The divers descended, but could find nothing. The waver runners from Bonheur 2 searched the shore—also fruitlessly. To make the emotional scene even grimmer, Albert's and Joey's girlfriends were on board as part of the crew.

Then the waters in which Bonheur 2 swung by one anchor began to roughen. Bonheur 2 would have to find a mooring in tiny Saba harbor, but such maneuvering was beyond Brody's competence. The certified captain of the deep-sea diving boat was invited to take over the Bonheur 2, and he successfully moored Bonheur 2 for the night.

The next day Brody hired a search plane but that too was futile. Brody hired another professional deep-sea diver from St. Martin's, and, he too could find nothing.

Brody and all aboard were interviewed by the police chief of Saba and permitted to leave. As they cruised past the site where Blair Albert was last seen, Bonheur 2 let out a forlorn whistle of mourning and goodbye. That night, Brody had the ghastly experience of telephoning all the relatives of Blair and Joey.

Brody had alerted the charter company in Ft. Lauderdale of the tragedy, and, in anticipation of the upcoming charter's leaving Antigua, they had already engaged a new captain. Brody tried to cancel the charter, but the charter party were intent on sailing. The charter party went forth with the cruise, and, in one of those cruel ironies, they wrote Brody a letter telling him what a perfectly wonderful time they had had.

Brody organized a memorial ceremony for Blair Albert in Ft. Lauderdale, which was well-attended, especially so by a large number of attractive young woman, who like most everyone else, had found Blair Albert irresistible.

In the coming years, Bonheur 2 would do most of her charter business in Europe, but like the first Bonheur, she never achieved the famous twenty weeks that would have made her a sustainable business investment. Brody had anticipated that the maintenance of Bonheur 2 would be relatively low, because she was brand new, but that expectation proved wrong. Even Bonheur 2's main engine needed replacement. Despite the charter revenue, Bonheur proved to be an enormous expense. Brody remembers that whenever he had a call from his accounting firm their first sentence was, "Jerry, tell me you've sold the yacht." Eventually, in 1998, he did.

Adorable Micol

V isitors to Gallagher's Stud are invariably impressed by the chapel-sized poolhouse attached to the Brodys' 18th-century wood-framed farm residence. Brody will tell you, "That is the poolhouse Allez Milord built."

1987 had been the best financial year for Gallagher's Stud. The Angus dispersal sale had fetched more than $1 million. The Yoshida Japanese syndicate had paid $1.3 million for Allez Milord and to that sum, Brody added $700,000 of Allez Milord's stakes winnings. Adorable Micol was winning in Europe and, at the suggestion of François Boutin and under the superb training of Ron McAnnaly, Adorable Micol had raced in California and her purses amounted to more than $250,000. The sons and daughters of Morning Games were in expensive demand.

1987 was also the year that Adorable Micol was retired from racing, with the very reasonable expectation that she would be the mother of champions. With her regal racing lineage and racing accomplishments, Brody was able to breed Adorable Micol to Lyphard, a Northern Dancer-Riverman cross. It was a mating with every chance of producing a great horse, and, if the logic of genes prevailed over bad luck, Brody would have his champion.

The odds had never been better.

The first filly out of Adorable Micol was Adoryphar, in whom the Brodys sold a fifty percent, $50,000 interest to Virginia Payson. Adoryphar, among her other prominent victories, established a new course record at Saratoga for the mile-and-three-eighths. But what should have been a rewarding and joyous experience for the Brodys turned bitter when Mrs. Payson's erratic insistence on her misunderstood prerogatives produced embarrassing conflict between the partners. Payson sued Brody, and Brody, eventually, wanting nothing more to do with Mrs. Payson, sold his interest for much less than it had become worth in light of Adoryphar's excellent performances.

The triumphant year of 1987 made the unprepossessing results of the next few years frustrating. There were winners and there were satisfactory sales, but the magic of Allez Milord and Adorable Micol could not be repeated. Adoryphar briefly whetted an appetite that remained unfulfilled. Brody wanted a racing champion badly.

In 1990, Adorable Micol was bred to the great Alydar, and the filly they produced was the very successful Adorydar. She finished second in the Group 1 Fantasy in Hot Springs Arkansas and was then shipped to California, winning several stakes races before finishing second in the Group 1 Santa Ana.

As a four-year-old, Adorydar started tapering off; she lost races she should have won. Perhaps, she has been raced too hard. Rather than risk her health by continuing to race her, Brody made the difficult decision to ship her to a breeding farm in Kentucky. Adorydar would not fulfill her early promise of racing greatness.

Brody dispatched Phil Trowbridge to Kentucky to take a look at Adorydar, who Trowbridge had not seen in two years. Word had come to Gallagher's Stud that Adorydar was quite thin, but what greeted Trowbridge's eyes distressed him more than weight loss. Trowbridge felt that something was seriously wrong with her.

Trowbridge returned to Gallagher's Stud, making an appointment to visit Adorydar again in two weeks. The next time Trowbridge saw her she had deteriorated further, and Brody and Trowbridge decided to bring her back to Gallagher's Stud.

In the meanwhile, Brody and Trowbridge began research and sought various diagnoses from the best available experts in the world. None of the veterinarians could give a conclusive diagnosis. Brody brought her back to the farm, and eventually consulted with his own personal physician, Dr. Albert Knapp. The medication Dr. Knapp prescribed appeared to stop the progression of whatever she had for about three months. But none of those consulted could give a precise diagnosis.

In December of 1993, two days before Christmas, the Brodys hosted the annual Christmas party for the farm family, neighbors, and friends. Only Brody did not come down from his bedroom. He was very sick. All day, Trowbridge stood by Adorydar in her stall. At the party, Trowbridge made a brief report to Brody and made another midnight check on Adorydar.

The next morning, when Trowbridge checked on her, she looked as if she would die. Trowbridge knew he had to tell Brody right away. Brody's sickness would not be an allowable excuse for Trowbridge to delay making full disclosure. Trowbridge gave Brody the news while Brody was flat on his back in bed. Trowbridge said. "We are in real trouble with this mare. What do you think we should do?" Brody, answering with much difficulty, said, "Do whatever you want to do." Brody turned away.

Trowbridge immediately left the sick man's room and rushed to the phone to call his wife, Ann, a registered nurse. He urgently said, "We had better get Mr. Brody to the hospital.

He has never ever told me to do whatever I want to do. Never. Not once. This man is real sick."

Marlene and Ann Trowbridge rushed Brody to the hospital, where Ann Trowbridge worked. Phil Trowbridge immediately rushed Adorydar to Tufts, where surgeons removed thirty feet of malignant intestines. She was dead in two days. The autopsy showed that Adorydar had had malignant lymphoma. Within two weeks, Brody, shaken and weak, was back on his feet, but the death of Adorydar was a severe emotional and financial blow to the Brodys.

Adorable Micol was Gallagher's Stud-bred and a proven broodmare and racehorse. Alydar went on to become one of thoroughbred racing's great sires. Adorydar, as a racing filly and as a broodmare might have been worth millions. Her colts could have been champions.

But out of tragedy there was to be a rebirth from Adorable Micol's indomitable genes. Phil Trowbridge thought that a curse hung over Adorable Micol when Adorable Micol, who had been bred to Storm Cat, a dominant stallion, was about to deliver her foal. Adorable Micol could not get the baby out. The situation grew desperate.

The previous spring Trowbridge had been in Kentucky for the yearling sales. Encouraged by Brody to seek the acquaintance of the best veterinarians in the business, Trowbridge had seen Dr. Rolf Embertson deliver a recalcitrant foal by hanging up the mother by her hind legs. Brody, previously having heard of such an emergency procedure, had ordered that such a lift mechanism be installed in the foaling barn, the first barn built at Gallagher's Stud. As a last ditch measure, it worked about one in a hundred times without killing either or both of the horses.

As Adorable Micol's protracted labor threatened her life and her foal's, Brody and Trowbridge decided to hang Adorable Micol by her hind feet. Thus Adcat was born and Adorable Micol emerged perfectly fit. Phil Trowbridge called it "a miracle."

Adcat's pedigree was such that Brody might have sold him for $1 million. Instead, he sold a one-third interest to Caesar Kimmel for $184,000, whose son, John Kimmel would train Adcat.

Out of the Ashes

Early in the morning of January 24, 1994, Bryan Reidy, the manager of Gallagher's, phoned Brody to inform him that there had been a serious fire at the restaurant. There had been a bad fire at Gallagher's in the 1970s. This one was worse.

Brody arrived, in his winter overcoat, brown fedora, a blue suit and a striped tie. Reidy led him into the still smoldering restaurant, which was teeming with fire fighters. Brody turned to his young manager and said, "Jesus, Bryan, can't you get rid of some of the fire trucks. They're causing a hell of a scene."

While Reidy, just immigrated from Ireland, was thinking that he had been manager of Gallagher's for only eighteen months and that he had seen the chance of a lifetime go up in smoke, Brody said to him, "Bryan, what are you doing? Shouldn't you be on the phone calling suppliers and construction people? Come on now, let's get back inside and get this place in order."

Reidy had the fire chief escort him back into the smoldering office so that he could get his telephone book. Reidy, who had just returned from a two-day visit to Mexico, had a good friend, in the construction business in Queens, a fellow Irish American. "Gallagher's has had a bad burn and I need you in here right away." He told him to get together a gang willing to work around the clock. His friend seemed relieved and said "Oh Jesus, that's nothing. I thought immigration had you in Mexico."

Under Brody's leadership, the work went forward at warp speed. What needed to be thrown out and bought new was. Brody refused to wait for the insurance company who told him to do nothing for six days until they had had a chance to inspect the damage. Reidy told them that if they wanted to see the damage, they'd have to go to a dump in Staten Island, where it already had been carted.

Gallagher's was open for business eight days after the fire. The Fire Chief who had orchestrated the defense of the fire and who had predicted that Gallagher's would not open again for a year, came in on the second day they were open. He could not believe his eyes.

In the two years after the Gallagher's fire, Adcat gave signs of developing into a stakes champion. Trowbridge and Adcat had a special bond. Always strong-minded and feisty, Adcat was affectionately tame in Trowbridge's hands. In anybody else's he was a "bad boy." Trowbridge said he could have trained him to ride in the cab of the pick-up truck with him. But once Adcat was put into John Kimmel's hands, the reports of his meanness and uncontrollably bad temper marred his future. Under John Kimmel, in his first race, Adcat finished fourth. Trowbridge, who thought that Adcat had what it took to win the Kentucky Derby, was disappointed and suspicious. Brody, after looking over Adcat himself, reported to Trowbridge that "this horse is not happy." Trowbridge took a look for himself. He reported to Brody, "This horse is petrified."

Against the wishes of the Kimmel father-and-son owner-trainer team, Brody changed trainers. He put Adcat into the hands of young Mark Hennig. Like Bryan Reidy and Phil

Trowbridge to whom Brody had handed over great authority of major enterprises, to Brody Hennig's age was no barrier to trust. Brody ordered Trowbridge to visit Adcat once a week. Overnight, in the hands of Hennig, Adcat's personality changed. Fear turned to trust, anxiety to growing confidence.

Two months passed and Adcat had not returned to the races, despite the urging of the Kimmels who saw an asset lingering unexploited. Hennig would not race Adcat until he felt the colt had regained his confidence.

In his first race at Belmont, Adcat finished first. Hennig bided his time for Adcat's next appearance at Saratoga. There Adcat finished fourth; his big frame unsuited for the tight turns. In his next start at Belmont he won by four lengths.

That winter, the Brodys were in residence at Gallagher's Stud during the pre-Christmas season. The Brodys, as they did at least twice a day when in residence at the farm, inspected their stable of thoroughbreds in the company of Phil Trowbridge and his staff. Perhaps in Adcat, Gallagher's Stud would return to the big time winners' circles. But pleasant thoughts of Christmas at the farm and important stakes races were interrupted at 6:00 AM, December, 1998, by a telephone call reporting that a serious fire had engulfed the Oyster Bar and nearly destroyed it.

When Brody arrived at the Oyster Bar, the fire had nearly been extinguished. Charred wrecked furniture stood in pools of dirty water. The stench of smoke was everywhere. The restaurant was dark, but in the beams of the firemen's flashlights, Brody could see the 7,000 priceless Rafael Guastavino tiles which had crashed from the ceiling when the cold water from the firehoses streamed onto the superheated tiles. The tiles had turned the restaurant into a giant convection oven. Light fixtures, wiring, kitchen equipment—all had melted.

The fire had been battled by the local fire company, and not by the Metropolitan Transit Authority (MTA) fire company assigned to Grand Central Station. The MTA would prove to be a major obstacle to the rebuilding of the Oyster Bar and getting it open for business.

Brody's attorneys immediately studied his lease with the MTA and advised Brody that he was free to proceed immediately with the restoration without getting permission from the MTA. Dennis Kuhn, a well-known restoration architect and Howard Brandston, a world-renowned lighting designer joined Brody's team that day and got to work.

Brody gathered all his restaurant workers, members of Local 100, and suggested that they organize into a crew that would get to work immediately on the immense job of cleaning up. The union workers were eager to get the Oyster Bar back up and running. For Brody continuity was essential for customers and the staff. The sooner the Oyster Bar was back in back in business the better.

Brody was able to hire his regular union electrician and plumber to get to work immediately and was lucky find the carpenter and general contractor who had done the original panelling when Brody had taken over the Oyster Bar in 1974.

The job of replacing the Guastavino tiles was intimidating. Guastavino had also adorned the reception hall at Ellis Island, which had also been given landmark status. The New York Landmark Commission insisted that the replacement tiles be identical to the original ones and that they, the Landmark Commission, would personally oversee the installation of each and every tile.

Brody was able to identify a small tile factory outside Buffalo, New York, which was equipped to do the work. Phil Trowbridge, who had relatives in the Buffalo area, dispatched his cousin's husband, an influential man in the area, to prevail on the factory to execute Brody's order. True to their word, the Landmark Commission supervised the installation of each and every tile.

The separate Saloon area of the restaurant had been untouched as was the kitchen opposite the main kitchen which prepares the Oyster Bar's famous oyster stews. Brody's plan was to start serving immediately in the Saloon, augmenting the chowders and stews with a cold menu, which would take the restaurant through the summer. Within a matter of days, the Saloon was open for business, even though the main areas of the Oyster Bar looked like a bomb site.

Two weeks later, Nancy Marshall, chief of leasing for the MTA, and some Metro North engineers summoned Brody to a meeting at which they insisted that he stop everything he was doing—restoration and serving his customers—until he submitted and the MTA approved his plans for the complete rebuilding of the restaurant. Brody, anticipating bureaucratic obstinacy, had brought along Dennis Kuhn, whose plans were rejected because the MTA would not consider "piecemeal" submissions. The MTA threatened court action if the work of restoration continued and if the Oyster Bar continued to serve its customers. Brody ordered all work to continue.

Two weeks later, Brody was summoned to the Supreme Court of the State of New York. Brody once again brought with him Dennis Kuhn and the plans for the electrical engineering. His attorney was Carmi Rapport, Brody's good friend and neighbor from Hudson County. The MTA was represented by the firm of Robertson and Silverman. After hearing both sides, the presiding judge asked the MTA if they would like to withdraw their brief.

So, despite the best efforts of Brody's landlords, Brody continued to rebuild the Oyster Bar, while gradually expanding its open areas. The Oyster Bar was very much alive. But this vitality did not seem to please the construction unions, who were at work on the massive restoration of the rest of the Grand Central Station complex.

The construction unions objected to the clean-up work being done by the Oyster Bar's restaurant workers of Local 100, who were part of Brody's regular crew. Every one of the construction unions, intent on monopolizing the work on the Oyster Bar for their own membership, sent his shop steward to visit Brody to register their complaint. Brody would not be intimidated. Nonetheless, when the entire restoration was almost completed, at 7:00 AM, the electricity feeding the Oyster Bar went out. Later that day, Brody's electricians discovered that the main feeder cables in the sub-basement had been cut in a very professional manner. The perpetrators were never found.

Brody's biggest problem with the Landmarks Commission involved the chandeliers newly designed by Howard Brandston. When the original chandeliers melted, Brody saw an opportunity to create a better design that lit the room more efficiently and beautifully. Because the new chandeliers could not be described as a restoration, Brody needed to appear before the Landmarks Commission to plead his case. In his plea, to which Brody's architects and lighting people gave high marks, Brody pointed out that Cornelius Vanderbilt, who had built Grand Central Station, was a man of the sea, and that these new chandeliers, which were adorned with accurately researched models of the fishing boats that plied New York waters when Grand Central was first built, would honor Vanderbilt's vision.

Brody was twice more summoned before the Landmarks Commission, and it was another year before the new chandeliers were approved. Nonetheless, the Landmarks Commission sent Brody a letter of high praise and shortly thereafter hosted a

Landmarks Commission cocktail party under those beautiful chandeliers against which they had so recently waged a stubborn battle. The MTA, whose architects, engineers and designers had first inspected the drawings for the chandeliers, had warned Brody that he would never get approval for them.

ESOP Fables

Perhaps seeing the revitalized Oyster Bar rise from the ashes of the fire made Brody turn his mind to the future of Gallagher's and the Grand Central Oyster Bar and to the legacy he would leave. Brody knew that very few restaurants survived the death of the original owner. And, Brody admitted to having the kind of ego that balked at oblivion.

Brody had already seen once in his lifetime his celebrated accomplishments at Restaurant Associates and, most notoriously, the Four Seasons, taken from him by family dissension and the self-serving historical revisionism of Joe Baum. He knew what it was to see the work of decades wiped from the public record. After his dismissal from RA, Brody had jumped back into the business after only a two-months' absence, and had singlehandely raised Gallagher's from decay and imposed his brand of management on it so that it was an almost instant success.

The same had been true at the Oyster Bar, bankrupt locked, and closed. Brody had revived it and turned it into the most famous seafood restaurant in New York, if not in America. And both restaurants had become evergreens, able to prosper far beyond ordinary life expectancy. Gallagher's and the Grand

Central Oyster Bar were Brody's creations, and he didn't want them to change or himself to be forgotten. Both restaurants were laboratory-pure examples of how his changes had made the difference between failure and success. Working out of the same location, with largely the same decor, by improving service, food quality, business controls, and marketing, Brody had turned two moribund operations into vital, profitable institutions.

Brody knew that he would have no trouble in selling either restaurant, but, if he were to sell out, how soon would it be before the restaurants would lose the distinctive excellence he and his key managers had worked so hard to achieve? Not only that, but were Brody to surrender control, he would be leaving his key personnel to the vagaries of the marketplace, and he felt that it would be inexcusable to reward their loyalty that way.

One potential buyer for the Grand Central Oyster Bar offered a very generous sum, with the proviso that Brody dismiss his old employees so that the new owners could take on the union and hire non-union personnel. In addition, the prospective new owner's wife had new decorating ideas that would substantially change the look of the Grand Central Oyster Bar. Brody was not surprised at such behavior and would have nothing to do with it.

Brody had long recognized the potential profitability of franchising. Now, with thoughts of establishing succession occupying his thoughts, the time was ripe. With the franchisee required to maintain the standards of the parent institution, Brody's vision would continue to inform and nurture a growing constellation of Brody-inspired restaurants.

Michael Weinstein, a friend of Brody's, controlled Ark Restaurants, the prestigious and successful restaurant company, a public company, which, among other properties, took over ownership of Lutéce from the legendary André Soltner. Ark had gained all the food and beverage concessions for a hotel in Las

Vegas, which was under construction, and which was to be called "New York New York." The owners of the hotel wanted to establish an authentic New York steak house and came to Brody with the idea of creating a Las Vegas Gallagher's at their casino site. Brody said he was interested, but only if the deal were a franchise operation in which Brody could enforce stringent quality controls. Ark's lawyers did everything in their power to make the deal as complicated as possible, but essentially it boiled down to two key ingredients. One, Ark agreed to the franchise arrangement and would pay Brody a fee and a percentage of gross. Two, Brody would exercise control over the appearance, style, and quality of the restaurant.

The restaurant opened at the same time as the casino and was an instant success. The first three years of the Las Vegas operation were notably successful, doing in excess of $7 million a year with only 140 seats (Gallagher's New York does $8.6 million with 330 seats). Brody did an on-site inspection of the operation and found only one element which he insisted be changed. New York New York was serving a sauce on the steak, which, to Brody, implied that the quality of the steak needed to be improved. The sauce was discontinued. Brody also felt that the table top was too fancy, too expensively presented, not in keeping with the New York Gallagher's style. But, with New York New York doing so well, Brody let that deviation from code slide.

The Las Vegas operation proved to Brody that a Gallagher's franchise had the ability to respond to marketing and promotion and that it could travel to all parts of the country. The next Gallagher's franchise opened in Princeton, New Jersey.

The success of the first two Gallagher's franchises proved what Brody had believed all along—that the Gallagher's name had substantial brand equity and that new franchises would respond vigorously to the marketing techniques he and his staff had developed over the course of many years.

Brody then turned his attention to the destinies of the New York Gallagher's and Grand Central Oyster Bar. Two separate concepts would form the basis of Brody's strategy: franchising and ESOP.

Brody would franchise Gallagher's and the Oyster Bar, but not to outside interests. This time Brody's key personnel would eventually become the owners of the newly franchised New York Gallagher's and Grand Central Oyster Bar. Brody would retain the right to establish other franchises wherever he wished,

In discussions with his long-time attorney friend from Hudson County, Carmi Rapport, Brody developed plans to offer the New York Gallagher's and Oyster Bar franchises to his key employees under the terms of tax legislation created by the congress called Employee Stock Ownership Plan (ESOP). Impartial appraisers would put a fair value on the business, which would have to be approved by the IRS. The key employees who became part of the ESOP would soon acquire ownership of Brody's stock in the restaurants out of the cash flow of the already profitable businesses.

The benefits were several—both to the newly enfranchised employees and to Brody and his estate. The employees would not have to come up with the millions needed to buy out Brody. Brody in turn would benefit from various tax advantages the ESOP payments would offer.

It was a relief when the complex ESOP plan was finally approved by the IRS and by the key personnel. But Brody did not mark the occasion by sitting back in his easy chair. He immediately made plans to establish the new corporate headquarters of the Gallagher's Steak House and Grand Central Oyster Bar Franchising Corporation in Miami, Florida. The hiatus between Brody's dismissal from RA and his purchase of

Gallagher's had been only two months. His establishment of the new Gallagher's and Grand Central Oyster Bar Franchise Corporation did not take that long.

A Marvelous View
of the Harbor

When Brody left for Miami in the winter of 1999, the first results of the transformation of the Grand Central Oyster Bar were becoming available. It appeared that business at the already successful restaurant seemed on the way to tripling. Potential franchisees would find the prospect of replicating Brody's restaurant models extremely attractive.

The Brodys moved south for the winter season of 1999. They vacated their two-bedroom condominium at the Jockey Club on Miami's Biscayne Bay and moved into a beautiful waterfront estate, that sits on a large, palm-shaded lawn with a wraparound view of Biscayne Bay and the Miami skyline.

The ostensible reason for leaving the Jockey Club was that the condominium board of the Jockey Club did not welcome the Brody's treasured standard French poodle, Rocky, who Marlene had rescued from a dog pound. But, with Brody's ability to travel back and forth to New York now restricted by a chronic lung ailment, the time was propitious to establish a permanent warm weather residence.

In less than a month of looking, the Brodys' found a bayfront estate with commanding views of Biscayne Bay. Knowing that he had come across a remarkable property, Brody closed the deal immediately.

The previous owner of the home had been an avid sailor. He had constructed the interior staircases, beams, floors, cabinetry and fixings to evoke the interior of a luxury yacht. A private docking area abutting the lawn is capable of handling anything from a runabout to a major offshore yacht. Seated before the panoramic bay windows, it is not impossible to imagine that one is on the captain's deck of Bonheur 2.

The Brodys have been reunited with Max Putier, their chef from the days of L'Étoile. Putier, who still thinks that Brody is the best restaurateur that America has produced, prepares dinner several times a week and acts as steward and estate manager. The comptroller of the New York Gallagher's, Frank Sblendido, has moved to Miami and has his office on the premises, handling the multitude of financial details of Brody's businesses and investments.

Throughout the day, Brody stays in touch with the New York restaurants and Gallagher's Stud by phone and fax. Each day he pours through financial data and status reports sent him by his executives. Now that the ESOP plan is in effect for Gallagher's New York and the Grand Central Oyster Bar, much responsibility is shared with his key managers, but Brody is still involved with all aspects of the restaurant operations. He is a part of all key decisions. It has just been decided that the Oyster Bar, whose already booming business has gone stratospheric since the remodeling of Grand Central Station, will for the first time in its history, be open on Saturdays for dinner.

Brody has put the development of new franchise opportunities into the hands of Brian Gallaghan, who was recommended for the job by Bryan Reidy. After seven months without landing a new franchisee, Gallaghan finalized a deal for a Gallagher's in

Denver. In short order, a deal was signed for a Grand Central Oyster Bar in Kansas City. Finally, the franchise business was taking off.

Negotiations are underway for a Gallagher's in Tampa and Atlanta and a Grand Central Oyster Bar in Tokyo. Cushman-Wakefield's Miami office is actively seeking a site appropriate for a Miami Gallagher's.

In the summer months, Brody and Marlene will return to Gallagher's Stud where the preceding season was the most successful in the breeding history of the farm. At the July 1999 yearling sales at Keenland, four Gallagher's Stud colts fetched $1.5 million, which included $900,000 for a colt by Seattle Slew out of Appealing Missy.

To have four colts selected for the auction by the Keenland experts was in large part due to the magnificent condition the animals were in when they were viewed by the Keenland inspection team before the Keenland sales. Phil Trowbridge had discovered a small, high-altitude farm whose winter hay tested at twenty percent protein, and bought out the entire supply. Neither Brody nor Trowbridge are giving out any information as to where this farm is located.

Just as the ESOP allowed Brody to address himself to the well-being of his key restaurant managers, Brody has made Phil Trowbridge a bequest of a portion of Gallagher's Stud farmland particularly admired by him.

At the November broodmare sales, also at Keenland, a group of Gallagher's Stud broodmares, led by the celebrated fifteen-year old Adorable Micol was sold—also for $1.5 million. Saying goodbye to Adorable Micol was particularly hard on Marlene, but she, too, knew the truth of the maxim that if you hold on to a broodmare too long, it is too late.

For Brody, the challenges still abound. The franchising

operation needs to be nurtured and an executive team trained and kept in motion. Brian Reidy is the president of the new franchise corporation while he still continues managing New York Gallagher's. Should the franchise corporation continue its growth, a new executive structure will have to be created. But as Brody says, he will cross that bridge when he comes to it.

The horse farm itself is a major operation, complex enough to justify Brody's full-time attention. But he will no longer be able to spend weekends there during the winter. The remodeling and furnishing of the new home is complex, expensive and time-consuming. Brody's best racehorses continue to come close to the highest levels, without reaching them—although on June 13, 1999 at Rockingham Park, in the $200,000 New Hampshire Sweepstakes, Grade 3, Adcat took home the $120,000 winner's purse.

As has been usual for the past fifty-five years, ever since he got out of the Army Air Force as a 24-year old bomber captain, Brody is taking care of business. But in the new Miami headquarters, with the living room walls covered with the magnificent paintings of Pierre Alechinsky, Jerry Brody and his adored wife Marlene look out over the sweep of Biscayne Bay and the Miami skyline gratified that business and pleasure have come close enough to join hands.

Index